242.2
WIL

Hope Notes
52 Meditations
to Nudge Your World

R. Wayne Willis

Westminster John K̲   ̲.̲ss

LOUISVILLE • LONDON

CONFERENCE RESOURCE LIBRARY
2517 North Main St.
North Newton, KS 67117

© 2004 R. Wayne Willis

All rights reserved. No part of this book may be reproduced or transmitted in any form or by any means, electronic or mechanical, including photocopying, recording, or by any information storage or retrieval system, without permission in writing from the publisher. For information, address Westminster John Knox Press, 100 Witherspoon Street, Louisville, Kentucky 40202-1396.

Scripture quotations, unless otherwise indicated, are from the New Revised Standard Version of the Bible, copyright © 1989 by the Division of Christian Education of the National Council of the Churches of Christ in the U.S.A., and used by permission.

Excerpt on p. 2 from "Oh, What A Beautiful Mornin'," Copyright © 1943 by WILLIAMSON MUSIC. Copyright Renewed. International Copyright Secured. All Rights Reserved. Used by Permission.

Excerpt on p. 2 from "You'll Never Walk Alone," Copyright © 1945 by WILLIAMSON MUSIC. Copyright Renewed. International Copyright Secured. All Rights Reserved. Used by Permission.

Excerpt on p. 2 from "A Cock-Eyed Optimist" by Richard Rodgers and Oscar Hammerstein II, Copyright © 1949 by Richard Rodgers and Oscar Hammerstein II. Copyright Renewed. WILLIAMSON MUSIC owner of publication and allied rights throughout the World. International Copyright Secured. All Rights Reserved. Used by Permission.

Book design by Sharon Adams
Cover design by Night & Day Design
Cover art by Teri Vinson

First edition
Published by Westminster John Knox Press
Louisville, Kentucky

This book is printed on acid-free paper that meets the American National Standards Institute Z39.48 standard. ∞

PRINTED IN THE UNITED STATES OF AMERICA

04 05 06 07 08 09 10 11 12 13—10 9 8 7 6 5 4 3 2 1

Library of Congress Cataloging-in-Publication Data

Willis, Wayne, 1942–
   Hope notes : 52 meditations to nudge your world / R. Wayne Willis—1st ed.
      p. cm.
   ISBN 0-664-22700-7 (alk. paper)
   1. Hope—Religious aspects—Christianity—Meditations. I. Title.

BV4638.W55 2004
242'.2—dc21

2003053775

To Dottie

My one true love—
After all these years,
And because of them,
I'm still crazy about you.

Hope Symbols

On a photography trip to Colorado several years ago, after witnessing a majestic sunrise, I asked the other three men for the first images that come to their minds when they heard the word *hope*. In no time, we came up with over fifty snapshots. That exercise confirmed for me how we humans are hardwired for hope—we look around us for visuals that lift up our hearts, that support our innate hopefulness. One of those fifty-two symbols, in the order in which it came to the four photographers in Colorado, introduces each chapter.

1. **anchor.** "We have this hope, a sure and steadfast anchor of the soul" (Heb. 6:19).
2. **arch.** We pass from death—through an Arch of Triumph—into eternal life.
3. **torch.** By a cloud in the daytime and a torch of fire at night, the Israelites were led out of the wilderness to the promised land.
4. **crown.** To those who compete well down in the arena there awaits a crown "which the Lord, the righteous judge, will give" (2 Tim. 4:8).
5. **dolphin.** This creature of the sea legendarily befriends humans and buoys up those drowning at sea.
6. **door ajar.** Through the open door one finds safety and hospitality, shelter and food.

7. **compass.** Knowing true north, we can make it over the sea or out of the forest.

8. **shepherd's crook.** God's "rod and staff" keep us out of the ditch, or help pull us out when we fall (Ps. 23).

9. **star.** When the clouds part, we can see the stars and find our way home.

10. **Bible.** Scriptures serve as "a lamp for our feet," lighting the way and keeping us on the path.

11. **eagle.** "Those who wait for the LORD shall renew their strength; they shall mount up with wings like eagles" (Isa. 40:31).

12. **musical note.** When we are afraid, we hum or whistle. "Music has charms to sooth a savage breast" (William Congreve).

13. **caduceus.** Two serpents criss-crossed around a shepherd's staff signify that a physician is near.

14. **newborn.** "A baby is God's opinion that the world should go on" (Carl Sandburg).

15. **acorn.** A seed is pure potential—inside is all the right stuff for evolving into a mighty oak.

16. **ship.** The castaway sees a sail on the horizon and takes heart—rescue is near.

17. **Earth.** Sight of the Big Blue Marble inspired astronauts coming from the dark side of the moon.

18. **vacancy sign.** There *is* room in the inn.

19. **Red Cross.** People of good will have pooled their resources—help is here.

20. **cap and gown.** We commence—new beginnings, new frontiers, new opportunities.

21. **oasis.** Salvation from scorching heat and parched lips—shade and water—is ahead.

22. **Statue of Liberty.** Upon arriving in the land of promise, millions have seen Lady Liberty and felt safe.

23. **H.** A hospital—help—is just ahead.

24. **lighthouse.** Its beacon will guide us through the straits and keep us from going on the shoals.

25. **life buoy.** "Throw out the lifeline across the dark wave—someone is sinking today."

26. **engagement ring.** We have the prospect of a companion for life's journey.

27. **hope chest.** Someday, my prince will come.

28. **fork.** Save your fork when the dinner plates are removed. Dessert—the best part—is yet to come.

29. **dawn.** We survived the dark night; we have lived to see another day.
30. **rainbow.** The rain will stop; the sun is coming out; the storm is over.
31. **butterfly.** An ugly, brown cocoon is not the final word.
32. **robin.** Winter gives way to spring.
33. **crocus.** "The winter is past . . . the flowers appear on the earth" (Song 2:11, 12).
34. **chimney smoke.** Someone is home. Tired and bedraggled, we'll be able to warm and dry ourselves by the hearth.
35. **St. Bernard.** Salvation is here in the form of a dog, sent by people searching for us.
36. **parachute.** We hope we'll never need to use it, but we're glad it's there—just in case.
37. **angel.** Angels' hands will bear you up, "so you will not dash your foot against a stone" (Matt. 4:6).
38. **cross.** "I have been crucified with Christ; and it is no longer I who live, but it is Christ who lives in me" (Gal. 2:19–20).
39. **icthus.** Christians scrawled the sign of the fish on catacomb walls. The Greek word for fish, *icthus*, was used as an acrostic for five Greek words: *Iesous* (Jesus), *Christos* (Christ), *theos* (God), *uios* (son), *soter* (savior).
40. **harp.** "Heavenly music leads us onward, in the triumph song of life."
41. **candle.** "Better to light a candle than to curse the darkness" (Adlai Stevenson).
42. **bridge.** You can get there—over troubled waters—from here.
43. **ladder.** Like Jacob, or John Bunyan's Christian in *Pilgrim's Progress*, we can climb. We can rise.
44. **hand.** "Precious Lord, take my hand, lead me on, help me stand."
45. **ripe fruit.** Mission accomplished.
46. **tetragrammaton.** Four Hebrew letters declare the mysterious, holy presence of God.
47. **Chi Rho.** The first two Greek letters of *Christos*, the Greek word for Christ.
48. **yellow ribbon.** May the missing one make it safely home.
49. **steeple.** Points us beyond the present, and the here, to the beyond.
50. **path.** Lost in the woods or jungle, how relieved we feel when a path appears!
51. **Christmas stocking.** Santa's coming!
52. **map.** With directions, we'll be able to get there.

Introduction

I'm stuck, like a dope,
With a thing called hope,
And I can't get it out of my heart!

I feel fortunate to have grown up in a generally hopeful era. The Great Depression had ended and vic-
torious American soldiers were returning from World
War II to enroll in college, marry, buy a house, raise a
family, and start a career—in other words, they were
ready to seize the American dream. Kids like me took to
heart what the Greatest Generation—parents and teachers, presidents and preachers—assured us was our mani-
fest destiny. Their message became my generation's
mantra: *The sky's the limit—you can become anything you
want to be.*

Even much of the music back then exuded hope. Oscar
Hammerstein II, then considered by many to be America's
poet laureate, was sometimes panned for composing lyrics
that were unduly hopeful. It was out of the depths of
World War II that he and Richard Rodgers conceived and
birthed the musical *Oklahoma!* Who can ever forget that

1

joyous opening scene? When the curtain rose, from off-stage, we heard the lone voice of a cowboy as he sang:

> There's a bright, golden haze on the meadow.
> The corn is as high as an elephant's eye,
> An' it looks like it's climbin' clear up to the sky.
> Oh' what a beautiful morning!
> Oh' what a beautiful day!
> I've got a beautiful feelin'
> Everythin's goin' my way.

In 1945, the war peaking in fury and atomic bombs exploding, Rodgers and Hammerstein wrote *Carousel*. One of the first songs I can remember humming or whistling around the house when I was little was from *Carousel*:

> When you walk through a storm,
> Hold your head up high,
> And don't be afraid of the dark.
> Walk on, walk on with hope in your heart,
> And you'll never walk alone.

In 1949, the arms race with the Soviet empire escalating and the future of the human race hanging in the balance, Rodgers and Hammerstein wrote *South Pacific*, based on a series of stories by James A. Michener. A line from one song that Rodgers and Hammerstein wrote for Nurse Nellie from Little Rock titled "Cock-Eyed Optimist" encapsulated their philosophy:

> I'm stuck, like a dope,
> With a thing called hope,
> And I can't get it out of my heart!

How much is due to early childhood influences like Hammerstein and how much to adult choices, I don't fully understand, but years ago I decided that my task on earth is to earn the epitaph HERE LIES A HOPE DOPE. The best use of my life I can think of, borrowing Jesse Jackson's phrase, is to "keep hope alive." If you've ever been on the receiving end—someone helped keep your hope alive when you were down for the count—I suspect you agree.

A couple of real or imagined near-death experiences taught me personally never to give up. Both times I could see no way out. Both times I thought I was a goner, literally going under for the third time. The first was in 1970 when I was canoeing with three friends on the Buffalo River in Arkansas. My canoe rode up a log in some rapids, we capsized, and I suddenly realized that I was trapped underwater in a tangle of logs. After maybe thirty seconds underwater, unable to find a way out, running low on air, the water pressure keeping me from going back to where I entered the log cage, I had one thought pounding in my head: "This is really it. This is no dream. I am actually drowning." Then, suddenly, I bobbed up and out. How, I'll never know.

My second near miss was in 1982, in the Atlantic Ocean off South Carolina. After an angry afternoon storm, I decided to go out alone for a swim. I was the sole soul out there. Floating on my back, enjoying my solitude and freedom, at some point I realized that my feet couldn't touch bottom. When I tried to stand, a strong undercurrent shoved my feet away from shore. I was alarmed to see that the shore was far, far away. I was being swept out to sea. There's an old cliché that at a time like your life passes before your eyes. Mine didn't. Instead, I had two thoughts. I wondered if they would ever find my body, or if sea creatures would dispose of it. And I remember realizing how angry and sad my wife and three little kids were going to be, having to drive back to Louisville, Kentucky, without me. About the time I started taking in water, giving up and going under from exhaustion, the undertow released me. The next day I read in the paper about a man several miles down the beach who foolishly, like me, went swimming about the same time I did. He had disappeared without a trace.

Those two experiences have ever since served to remind me that my perception of things is inevitably flawed. There are possibilities in any situation that I, looking out from my dark little cave, cannot see. Knowing that is always the case, I must never give up.

But more than any other one thing, the Judeo-Christian faith that came in with my mother's milk nurtured the formation of hope within me. Every Sunday morning, Sunday night, and Wednesday night my family went to church and dissected the scriptures. We started in Genesis and plodded through Exodus, examining it verse by verse, line by line, word by word. When we finished Exodus, we turned back to Genesis and started over again. That central story—the Israelites escaping Egypt and journeying toward the promised land, a cloud by day and a pillar of fire by night going before them and leading them onward—became my primary hope story. That theology posited a God going before and leading the way, beckoning and luring faithful followers into the future. When our searching the Scriptures occasionally reached the New Testament, there we read, times four—Matthew, Mark, Luke, and John—the Gospel's central story of Easter trumping Good Friday. My childhood faith was grounded in exodus and resurrection. As a child, I got a heady-with-hope theological inoculation.

Over the past quarter century, many hospital patients and their families have exquisitely modeled hope for me. They taught me far more about hope than I, their hospital chaplain, taught them. Many years ago, to give one example, a very special baby was born to a couple in rural Kentucky. Infertile for many years, mom and dad knew this baby would be the only one they could ever have. Angie was born with multiple problems, and after four months in our neonatal intensive-care unit—with at least one of her parents by her side every day, keeping watch and cheering her on—Angie died. Her parents asked me to conduct the funeral.

I arrived at the funeral home, embarrassingly just a few minutes before the service was to begin. The funeral director hurriedly told me it was one of the largest funerals they had had in that little town, so esteemed were the parents and so involved the whole community had been in praying and pulling for Angie. When I walked out into the packed house, my eyes instantly locked on the people filling the front two pews. I actually heard them before I saw them, because they were all sobbing. I knew them all. They were Angie's nurses, eight of them from the neonatal intensive-care unit in Louisville, sitting in solidarity with the family. They had taken the day off without pay, driven seventy-five miles to sit in the ashes and mix their tears with the tears of the bereaved parents they loved. There's an old Persian proverb I will always associate with that day: "You may forget with whom you laughed, but you'll never forget with whom you cried." For many years Angie's parents came to Louisville at Christmas time, bearing gifts of country ham for the nurses who had saved them from deep despair and kept their hope alive.

One of my favorite cartoons features a man gazing at a pile of smoldering ashes. The caption reads: "What I'll remember most about him was his indefatigable optimism." I write this book hoping that in some way one of these notes will help you, or someone you love, keep hope alive. Selfishly, I write it to work on that "hope dope" epitaph. All of us are dopes, or fools, for something—popularity, looks, success, sex, booze, money, fame—something. I aspire to be a hope dope.

I invite you, for one year, to journal your reflections on hope. Live with the quotation or the symbol or the commentary of each of the fifty-two chapters for a week. Mull the content over in the corridors of your mind. Write down how your thoughts and feelings and life experiences resonate with mine. You may feel moved, I hope, from time to time, to share your reflections with someone you trust.

Tom Stoppard wrote in his play, *The Real Thing*, that when writers get the right words in the right order, they can "nudge the world" a little. May one of these words help you, or someone you love, to nudge the world a little.

Chapter One

Who has seen the wind? Neither you nor I. But when the trees bow down their heads, the wind is passing by.

Christina Georgina Rossetti

What is real? A banana split is real. I have seen one. Better yet, I have tasted one. Seeing—and tasting—is believing.

White blood cells are real. Although they are invisible to the naked eye, under a microscope you can see white blood cells. You can even count them.

Some things that are very real can't be seen, even under an electron microscope. Like air. Or gravity.

Maybe matter is overrated. Most of what we call matter is really empty space. Matter is composed of atoms. Atoms are mostly empty space, with a few particles circulating in the empty space. The nucleus of the atom, as well as the protons and neutrons inside the nucleus, are largely empty space. The Rock of Gibraltar is primarily empty space. If all its empty space could be taken out, leaving only the matter, the Rock of Gibraltar's matter would fit inside a Ping-Pong ball. As Buckminster Fuller, one of the great architects of the twentieth century and inventor of the geodesic dome, wrote, "Everything you've learned in school as 'obvious' becomes less and less obvious as you begin to study the universe. For example, there are no solids in the universe."

Nonmaterial things matter. In the long run, they may matter *more* than matter. Consider hope, for instance. Is hope real? You can't measure it, weigh it, dissect it, photograph it, touch it, or taste it. You can't see it under the most powerful electron microscope. Is it real?

Come to the hospital and see. See parents watching for the surgeon to round the corner with news that their child's surgery is over and the child is safe. See the cardiac patient huffing and puffing on the treadmill. See the mother signing the consent for her two-year-old's bone marrow transplant. See the octogenarian learning to walk with her new hip. Is hope real? It is not only real—sometimes it's really the only thing that keeps us going.

Don't neglect nonmaterial things—like faith and hope and love. In the real world, they are huge. They matter more, in the long run, than all the matter in the world.

Use the space below to record your thoughts.

Chapter Two

I merely took the energy it takes to pout and wrote some blues.

Duke Ellington

Life's ultimate hope-crusher, most would agree, is the death of a child. Of his daughter Susy's death at age twenty-four, Mark Twain wrote: "It is one of the mysteries of our nature that a person, all unprepared, can receive a thunder-stroke like that and live."

Yet bereaved parents carry on. How?

After a thirteen-year-old girl was killed by a drunk driver in 1980, her mother and several other California mothers began MADD (Mothers Against Drunk Driving). Now hundreds of chapters strong, MADD has successfully lobbied for changes in laws that have saved thousands of lives.

After John Walsh's six-year-old son Adam was abducted and murdered in 1981, John began hosting "America's Most Wanted," a television program that located hundreds of missing children and led to the capture of hundreds of criminals.

After Rabbi Harold Kushner's young son died of progeria, a rare and always lethal condition, Kushner wrote *Why Bad Things Happen to Good People*, probably the most read and most helpful book ever written on grief.

When life mugs you, robs you of what you hold most dear, leaving you for dead, how can you keep your hope alive? You can use your loss to bless someone else whose wounds are fresher than yours.

Use the space below to record your thoughts.

Chapter Three

There is a fountain of youth: it is your mind, your talents, the creativity you bring to your life and the lives of the people you love.

Sophia Loren

Those who disprove old age stereotypes inspire us and pump up our hope. As we get older, we make them our role models.

Consider Sam Gadless. In his seventies, Sam had such bad arthritis that he couldn't lift one arm. He had to have bones in his big toes replaced with artificial ones. Sam developed an ulcer that required the surgical removal of half his stomach. His doctor told him his days were numbered. But Sam decided to start life over. Years later, in 1999 he competed in his eighth New York City marathon. He was, at age 92, the 26.2-mile race's oldest entrant. "Age is just numbers," Sam said. "When I was younger, I was sick as could be. I'm living my youth now."

Consider centenarian Frank Smith. Frank was a pipe smoker until he was well into his second century. He said he was able to quit the same way he quit drinking whiskey—one day he made up his mind to stop. "You can quit any of your habits if you want to," Frank explained. "You didn't have the habits when you were born, did you?"

When he was over ninety years of age, Supreme Court Chief Justice Oliver Wendell Holmes Jr. was hospitalized, and President Franklin Roosevelt paid him a visit. The president found him reading a Greek grammar. "Why, pray tell," the president asked, "are you reading a Greek grammar at your age?" Holmes replied: "To improve my mind, Mr. President."

To keep hope alive, we have to guard against ever letting a rigid old person take up residence in our body and do our thinking for us.

Use the space below to record your thoughts.

Chapter Four

And so from hour to hour we ripe and ripe, then from hour to hour we rot and rot, and thereby hangs a tale.

                                         William Shakespeare

Have you congealed yet? Do you know people who have? I've been around so many middle-aged and old people who have congealed that this is my number one fear.

Of congealing, Gail Godwin in *The Finishing School* wrote:

> There are two kinds of people. One kind you can just tell by looking at them at what point they congealed into their final selves. It might be a very nice self, but you know you can expect no more surprises from it. The other kind keep moving forward and making new trysts with life, and the motion of it keeps them young. In my opinion, they are the only people who are still alive. You must be constantly on your guard against congealing.

Some of us stay stuck in a rut because our dreams are too vague, too general. We hope to "have a good life" or "be happy" or "do better" or "get it together." Such non-specific dreams make it impossible to measure whether we're really making progress.

At the beginning of each year, Benjamin Franklin made a list of fifty-two virtues he wanted to cultivate or vices he wanted to eliminate in that calendar year. He focused on each one for one week.

Terri Fallin of Louisville, Kentucky, drew up a list of one hundred experiences she wanted to have in her lifetime (visit all fifty states, learn to windsurf, enter a photography contest, ride in a hot-air balloon, and more). Every year she gives herself a report card on how she's doing. What she illustrates is how the difference between a "pipe dream" and a realized goal is often a timeline.

How clearly defined are your hopes and dreams? Are you stagnating or "pressing on the upward way"? Are you ripening, or rotting?

Use the space below to record your thoughts.

Chapter Five

Hope has two daughters—anger and courage.
Augustine

Some people keep on keeping on, even when all hope is lost. How do they do that?

The Academy Awards' best foreign-language film of 1999, *Life Is Beautiful*, attempts an answer. Guido, an Italian Jew played by Roberto Benigni, and his five-year-old son have been warehoused in a Nazi concentration camp. Guido daily sees trucks and boxcars hauling away camp prisoners to the gas ovens. Knowing that the time of his extermination is near, Guido convinces his little boy that the whole thing is really an elaborate game, a contest that, if they play well, will reward them with the grand prize— an army tank of their own. Even as he walks off to his execution, Guido stays focused on modeling hope and joy for his boy. He plays the game out for one reason—to save his little boy's tender spirit from being crushed.

Viktor Frankl, one of the great psychiatrists of the past century, survived the horrors of those same ovens. One of his most unforgettable memories from the camps was of those men who, starving, gave others nearing death their last crusts of bread. How could they do that? Frankl said they were exercising their one unconquerable freedom—the freedom to choose which attitude to hold, regardless of circumstances. They chose to practice faith, hope, and love—to adopt a noble stance in dire straits—regardless of the outcome.

A seventy-five-year-old social activist in the hills of eastern Kentucky, when asked by Studs Terkel why he had not retired, gave his unflagging activism this defense: "I owe it to the people of this community. The last flicker of my life will be against something that I don't think has to be."

Why bear up, even when the odds are astronomically against us, even in the face of doom? Because others are looking to us. They are reading us, scanning our behavior for any clues to the meaning of life, and searching for any bit of guidance or hope.

Why bear up? Do it for the community. Do it, like Guido, for the kids.

Use the space below to record your thoughts.

Chapter Six

Never, never ever give up.
Winston Churchill

Sometimes it is impossible to see a good ending to the story.

Who, looking at an ugly brown cocoon, could ever imagine a beautiful monarch butterfly emerging? A cocoon bears no visual resemblance to a butterfly.

Who, looking at an egg, could ever imagine a magnificent eagle coming from it? An egg bears no earthly resemblance to an eagle.

Was there one earthling in 1943, in the depths of World War II, who foresaw that at the end of the twentieth century two of America's best friends in the world would be Japan and Germany?

In 1962, when "the evil empire" threatened to bury America, did one soul on planet Earth foresee that, before the century was out, the Soviet Union would disintegrate and descend into the desperation it knew at the turn of the millennium?

How many times in life could you not see any way out and, lo, there was one?

Dr. Karl Popper, a British philosopher of science, explains: "Knowledge is finite, but ignorance is infinite." We never can know enough to be hopeless. Or a pessimist. Or an atheist. There are possibilities that we, in our thick, dark little cocoons, simply cannot see.

Use the space below to record your thoughts.

Chapter Seven

The greatest danger for most of us is not that our aim is too high and we miss it, but that it is too low and we reach it.

Michelangelo

One September day when I was a teenager, a friend and I decided to make some money walking the shoulders and ditches of dusty Tennessee country roads, picking up discarded bottles and cans. Back then, cans and bottles brought a penny each. We didn't make much money that day, but I did find a pickle jar that I can still see in my mind. It was filled with a pumpkin. Surrounding the pint-sized pickle jar containing the pint-sized pumpkin was a field of beautiful, fully grown pumpkins, the size of basketballs and larger. A pumpkin vine had by chance put forth a blossom at the mouth of the pickle jar. The little pumpkin grew into the jar and filled it. Having conformed to the shape and size of the little jar, out of space to expand, the pumpkin stopped growing.

We are born, like that pumpkin, into a jar. Life's lottery imposes on each of us some ceilings and walls. They have names like gender, race, geography, poverty, an inadequate parent, an abusive parent, a birth defect—barriers that should stunt our growth and keep us from achieving our fullness. In spite of it all, some of us summon the wherewithal to burst out of the glass cage and keep on growing.

There's another jar, maybe even harder to break through than the one we inherit at birth—the jar we give ourselves. We erect ceilings and walls in our minds that keep us from achieving our fullness. We don't get around to saving for our dream vacation, don't get around to going back to school for our dream degree, don't get around to applying for our dream job, don't get around to asking out our dream date, don't get around to giving our body the regimen of exercise and nutrition it craves. We deny our dreams. We settle for mediocrity.

We are meant to become fully evolved persons. What a pity to let an old pickle jar deny us the dream.

Use the space below to record your thoughts.

Chapter Eight

In the midst of death hope sees a star, and listening love can hear the rustle of a wing.

Robert Ingersoll

A man came upon a guru sitting at the intersection of several roads.

"O wise man," he pleaded, "please show me the way to wisdom, meaning, and truth."

The guru pointed down one road. The man trotted off in that direction, full of anticipation. Just as he disappeared over the horizon there was a great "*Kaboom!*" The earth shook. There was a flash of light and a cloud of dust. The man shuffled back to the guru, disheveled and bewildered.

"I'm afraid there's been a mistake," he said. "I must have misunderstood your directions. I asked you to show me the way to wisdom, meaning, and truth."

The guru again said not a word but pointed in the same direction. This time the man walked away, slowly, more than a little apprehensive. Sure enough, as soon as he disappeared over the horizon, "*Kaboom!*" The earth shook.

There was a flash of light and a cloud of dust. He returned to the guru covered with debris and his clothes shredded.

"You fraud!" he angrily told the guru. "This is not funny! Twice I ask you for the way to wisdom, meaning, and truth and you don't even speak. You just point."

The wise man rose to his feet, pointed once more in the same direction, and spoke: "Wisdom, meaning, and truth beyond *Kaboom!*"

Most of us, by this point in the journey, know about "*Kaboom!*" We've sustained a divorce, a death, a diagnosis, an accident, a failure—some event that shattered illusions we may have had about being in control, being self-made, and being secure. But now we know that it was then— "*after Kaboom!*"—that we were most open to learning truth about life, best positioned to appreciate wisdom about life, and highly motivated to examine our values and search for meaning in life.

It was then—"*after Kaboom*"—that we learned how essentially dependent we are on others. The hands of others lifted us from the womb. Others' hands diapered and bathed us. Others' hands built the cars we drive, grow and harvest and deliver the food we eat, fix our teeth, empty our bedpans, and perform our bypass surgery. Others' hands lift us out of the rubble "*after Kaboom!*" Others' hands hold the bandages and ointments ready. Others' hands reach out and touch us when we're grieving, and steady us when we would wobble and fall. And others' hands will one day lower us into the grave.

We need each other, cradle to grave. Extend a hand. Accept a hand. Hold a hand. Keep hope alive—after *Kaboom!*

Take a few minutes to reflect on what you've just read.

Chapter Nine

When you have exhausted all the possibilities, remember this: you haven't.

Thomas Edison

What images do you associate with hope? A rainbow (sunshine following a rain)? A crocus or robin (winter giving way to spring)? A butterfly (beauty coming from an ugly cocoon)?

One of my favorite pictures of hope is artist George Frederic Watts's creation. He paints a woman blindfolded and curled in a fetal position over a sphere (representing the earth), a one-string lyre her only companion. All the other strings on the lyre are broken. Watts entitles this image of the woman plucking the one string she has left: "*Hope.*"

My favorite symbols of hope, the ones that spring first to my mind when I'm feeling low, are the faces—particularly the eyes—of children.

I see a little boy named Damon, age five, who wears thick glasses and a patch on one eye to treat his amblyopia. He presses on—oblivious to looks of pity he is getting from others—as if something deep inside is propelling him and whispering, "Go forward! Go forward!" He just knows that he wants to ride a scooter and slide down a slide and color pictures and grow up.

I see a little boy named Forrest, age seven, with orthopedic braces on both legs. He waddles along—slowly, uncomfortably, clumsily, noisily. He endures stares and hears catcalls almost every day. But some powerful, mysterious, life-loving force urges him onward.

I see a little ten-year-old girl named Danielle. She is bald from chemotherapy. Nevertheless, when her eyes meet mine, she smiles sweetly and speaks. Doesn't she know fate has robbed her of her youth and may rob her of her life? Doesn't she understand how cruelly life has double-crossed her?

Next time you feel you're at the end of your rope, download a child's hope-filled face, tie a knot, and hang on.

Use the space below to record your thoughts.

Chapter Ten

The journey is better than the inn.

Cervantes

Arguably the greatest basketball team of all time was the 1995–1996 Chicago Bulls. Coached by Phil Jackson and led by Michael Jordan, the Bulls won seventy-two games and the NBA championship.

The secret to their successful season, according to coach Jackson, was a sentence. The team adopted the sentence before the season began. They agreed—to a man—to bet the season on it. Their sacred sentence: *The Journey Is the Reward.*

To live mindfully—to pour ourselves into the task at hand, to concentrate fully on the needs of the moment—makes meaning for a day. "If I drink oblivion of a day," George Meredith warned, "so shorten I the stature of my soul." Our souls either grow a little or shrink a little every day. When we take care of soul business one day at a time, when we live in what Eckhart Tolle calls "the power of now," how the journey ends has a way of taking care of itself.

John Wooden, legendary UCLA basketball coach, won more national championships than any other college coach in history. Once he was asked if, in his retirement, he missed coaching. "I miss the practices, but I don't miss the games," Wooden said. "I agree with Cervantes: 'The journey is better than the inn.'"

Are we fooling ourselves when we think life begins after we leave home, after we get married, after we have children, after we earn our degree, after we start the next job, after we get the big promotion, after we buy the next house, after the kids leave home, after we retire?

As award-winning author of children's books, Ursula K. Le Guin wrote: "It is good to have an end to journey toward, but it is the journey that matters in the end."

Use the space below to record your thoughts.

Chapter Eleven

I live on food and dreams. Give me mostly dreams.

Jesse Stuart

We cannot live, Jesus said, on bread alone.

Jesse Stuart would agree. He grew up hungry in a hollow in Greenup, Kentucky. His home was located so deep in the hills that the hoot owls, mistaking day for night, would sometimes holler in the daytime. When Jesse eventually made it to Vanderbilt University with little more than the clothes on his back, he survived on eleven meals a week. He tanked up on water before going to class. Then during class he would sit with his elbow pressed into his stomach, trying to keep his stomach from growling and embarrassing him.

By the time of his retirement, Jesse Stuart had written thirty-two books and four hundred short stories. He had accepted invitations to give over five thousand lectures around the world. In 1954, Kentucky named him poet laureate of the commonwealth.

Jesse Stuart determined early in life, plowing on a Kentucky hillside, the place that physical hunger would play in his life. In his autobiography, *To Teach, To Learn*, he writes:

> I always felt sorry for the mule. He pulled the plow, and I only guided it through the roots. He knew as much about plowing as I did. I didn't have to drive him. A mule knows right where to step. But he can't tell his driver whether he is hungry or not. And food, for the mule, is all he lives for. Give it to him. I don't live for food alone. I live on food and dreams. Give me mostly dreams. Cramp your guts when they growl. Push them against your backbone with your hand flat against your stomach. But don't cramp your dreams.

Our "muleness" is a given. And it is a gift. Animal instinct—muleness—drives us, as it does the mule, to find food and shelter, to persevere, to survive. But our humanness, unlike the mule, craves more than survival. We alone, in the animal kingdom, aspire. We aspire to evolve higher, to become more than we are, to exploit the gifts God gave us. We aspire to write things worth reading or to do things worth writing about. We aspire to right some wrongs, to make someone else's load a little lighter, or to leave things a little better than we found them.

The mule, according to the proverb, prefers garbage to gold. We have to guard against settling into the mule-like rut named "just getting by" or "just surviving." As Jesse Stuart admonished, "Cramp your guts when they growl . . . but don't cramp your dreams!"

Take a few minutes to reflect on what you've just read.

Chapter Twelve

No person is so lost that eternal love cannot return, so long as hope retaineth ought of green.

Dante

Deep in February, when the ground is brown and the trees barren, when the earth looks dead as a door-nail, I sometimes scratch a branch on one of my peach trees with my thumbnail. I'm anxious to see if the branch is brown through and through—dead. It sure looks dead. Usually I'm relieved to find bright green concealed beneath the dull brown. And I take heart, knowing the buds will soon begin to swell. Then another few weeks and a speck of green will appear at the tip of the bud. There surely will be another spring!

When I find myself wondering how many years of life I have left, I think in terms of how many springs I have left to enjoy. That may be an almost universal experience—as winter defers to spring, our souls clap hands and sing.

Once when a young man I know well was going through a hard time, a friend mailed him a note that contained this quotation (by an unknown composer): "Always keep a green branch in your heart. Someday a bird will come and perch on it and sing for you."

We all have our winters, our long, dark nights of the soul. The landscape is brown and the sky is gray. We're running low on hope. It's hard to remember then, when it's bleak as bleak can be, the faithful law of nature—winter surely surrenders to spring.

When we're frozen in a wintry mode, and our landscape looks cold and barren, and hope is growing thin, we can make Charles Spurgeon's words our daily prayer: "Lord, end my winter, and let my spring begin."

Use the space below to record your thoughts.

Chapter Thirteen

My knowledge is pessimistic, but my willing and hoping are optimistic.

Albert Schweitzer

What to do, when our best-laid plans get suddenly and unexpectedly interrupted? The most admired person in the world half a century ago may hold the answer.

Albert Schweitzer earned four doctorates early in life—one in philosophy, one in theology, one in music, and one in medicine. In his early thirties, wooed by the world's great universities and seminaries and medical schools, Schweitzer turned his back on the prestige and security of an academic career in Europe to become a jungle doctor in Africa. Caring for the sick masses in Africa became his passion for the next half century.

Just several years after beginning his work in Africa, worldwide war broke out. Albert Schweitzer and his wife were placed on a ship and sent as prisoners of war to a camp in Europe. How would the distinguished doctor cope, having had his status diminished to prisoner of war?

In his autobiography, *Out of My Life and Thought*, Schweitzer described "the manifold misery that prevailed in the camp." Daily he observed despairing prisoners who "kept walking round and round looking out over the walls at the glorious white shimmering chain of the Pyrenees. They no longer had the stamina to occupy themselves with anything. When it rained, they stood about apathetically."

Schweitzer, by contrast, busied himself with learning. He wrote:

> No books were needed in the camp to improve one's education. For everything one might want to learn, there were men with specialized knowledge at one's disposal, and from this unique opportunity for learning I profited greatly. About finances, architecture, factory building and equipment, grain growing, furnace building, and many other things, I picked up information I could probably never have acquired elsewhere.

All the prisoners shared similar circumstances—life interrupted, freedom denied, future unknown. The common and understandable response was to disengage and stare despairingly at the distant mountains. Schweitzer chose to engage—interview others, listen carefully, absorb their knowledge, and acquire their wisdom. That activity helped keep his own hope, as well as the hope of others, alive.

What to do when our life plans get interrupted, perhaps by a hospitalization, or a divorce, or an unwelcome job change? Hope begs us to ask if there might possibly be a gift—some personal growth, some spiritual insight, some opportunity to learn something invaluable—disguised as an interruption.

Take a few minutes to reflect on what you've just read.

Chapter Fourteen

Facts are like cows: if you look them in the face
hard enough, they generally run away.

Dorothy Sayers

Like *Dragnet*'s Joe Friday, we want "just the facts." But "the facts" shift and change. Just a few centuries ago, that the earth was the center of the universe, and flat, was a fact. Remember when everyone told you it was a known fact that you couldn't do something, and you did? Think of all those people who were told by significant people in their life that they would never amount to anything, and they did. Remember when the scientifically sound breakfast, the one that physicians recommended, the one that would make you healthy, wealthy, and wise, was bacon and eggs and buttered white toast and whole milk?

"Facts" change. It's one thing to face (what seem to be) the facts, and another to accept them as absolute, inviolable, set-in-concrete, good-for-all-time reality. We must resist being bound and determined and intimidated by what appear at one time to be the facts.

Norman Cousins, *Saturday Review* editor and a member of the University of California, Los Angeles (UCLA) medical school faculty, twice had his physicians deliver to him the fact that he was terminally ill. Twice he survived their predictions. Cousins passed on this wisdom to patients who are given doom-and-gloom news: "Don't deny the diagnosis. But do defy the verdict."

Hope faces the facts. Then hope works like crazy to change the facts. And if the facts can't be changed, hope aims to make something positive happen in spite of the facts.

Use the space below to record your thoughts.

Chapter Fifteen

People are determined, not by things, but by the views they take of them.

Epictetus

A wise woman once charged high school seniors, as they were poised to graduate and go forth into the world, "What I tell you today you must never forget. To every person is given the key to the gate of heaven. But know this—the same key also opens the gate to hell."

Five forces come together to account for how we each use our one key—to open the gates of heaven, or to open the gates of hell.

1. *Constitution*. Each of us enters the world with a one-of-a-kind temperament or predisposition. Our personality is shaped by the genetic material contained in our father's seed and mother's egg.

2. *Culture*. Each of us grows up at a particular address. The soil in the neighborhood—very rocky or very fertile or somewhere in between—influences how we turn out.

3. *Cultivation.* If our soil doesn't get cultivated, we may not even survive. How well our ground is weeded and worked by family and teachers and others affects what we become.

4. *Climate.* Each of us has to contend with different weather. Chance gives some of us a fortuitous balance of sunshine and rain; others get cruel storms and hailstones, floods and droughts.

5. *Choice.* In many people, this fifth force—unique to Homo sapiens—overrules and dominates the other four.

We choose to be (or not to be) hopeful—regardless of what our parents were like, regardless of where we grew up, regardless of how much help we got along the way, regardless of the slings and arrows of outrageous fortune. The key to hope or hopelessness, to heaven or hell, we hold in our hand.

Use the space below to record your thoughts.

Chapter Sixteen

I was led oftener through the Realm of Briar than the Meadow Mild.

Emily Dickinson

For some of us, hope was born and bred in a meadow. We learned hope in the summer, under cloudless, friendly skies. As far back as we can remember, it was easy to believe in God, to believe that life is good and people are good and that "you can become anything you want to be." Frowners and whiners were and are a puzzlement to us. Browning captured the "meadow mild" view of the world when he wrote, "God's in his heaven, and all's right with the world."

Hope, for others of us, was forged in—or in spite of—a briar patch. Life has been a struggle all the way. Scratched and scarred, we nevertheless press on, hoping against hope to reach a clearing someday. "Why me, God?" is a frequent prayer. Occasionally we feel a twinge of envy or resentment toward the Pollyannas around us who don't know or understand—and can't appreciate—what we've been through.

To the briar people, meadow-hope looks superficial, naive, fragile, easy, thin.

To the meadow people, briar-hope looks jaded, gnarled, compromised, cynical, weak.

We are drawn to those whose hope came like ours. We identify with them, are compatible with them, and feel comfortable with them. They are kindred spirits. The trick is to be charitable toward—and rejoice with—those who got theirs the other way.

Use the space below to record your thoughts.

Chapter Seventeen

Call me trim tab.
Buckminster Fuller

Occasionally I hear a nurse or some other health-care worker say something like this: "It's so frustrating, trying to make a difference when surrounded by so much misery. I feel little and insignificant. Some days it feels like I am one person trying to empty the ocean with a spoon."

Sighs of frustration like that remind me of the epitaph on Buckminster Fuller's tombstone. Fuller invented the geodesic dome and is widely regarded as one of the most innovative architects of the twentieth century. Toward the end of his life, he made his heirs promise to engrave on his cemetery marker, under his name and birth date and death date, four words: *Call me trim tab.*

A trim tab is a small rudder that is attached to the large rudder of a ship or airplane. The tiny trim tab does very little. All it can do is nudge the rudder a little. But it does move the rudder, and the rudder in turn changes the course of a giant ocean liner or jumbo jet.

Buckminster Fuller understood his place in the scheme of things. He accepted the fact that in life there are very few rudders—giants who change the course of history. The rest of us are bit players. Our part in the great drama called life is minor, but, like the trim tab, not insignificant.

We each nudge the world a little. What is important, for Buckminster Fuller and for the rest of us, is in which direction we give our nudge.

Use the space below to record your thoughts.

Chapter Eighteen

Just give hope a chance to float up, and it will.
Steve Rogers

Do you believe in voodoo? Does voodoo really work?

In the second quarter of the last century, Walter Cannon, Harvard physiologist and world-class authority on how the body works, was asking that question. Travelers from around the world had brought him many tales of witch doctors who cast a magic spell on a person, and that person died by sundown. So Cannon closely examined the stories that came from Australia, New Zealand, Haiti, Brazil, and Africa. He studied the testimonies of eyewitnesses and autopsy findings.

His conclusion? Voodoo really works! Perfectly healthy specimens, hexed by the medicine man, died within a short period of time. The autopsies revealed that no poisons were involved and no trauma was used. Cannon's conclusion? "A fatal power of the imagination" took possession of the cursed man. He believed he was lost and undone—that there was no way out. That hopelessness translated into the man's cells and tissues and organs and shut him down.

Hopelessness is a killer. It can make you sick. It's as life-threatening as poison or trauma. It can make you dead.

Hope, on the other hand, is a strengthening force. It refuses to goose-step with the forces arrayed against it that would intimidate and destroy it.

The witch doctor goes out of business when he points his magic bone and the would-be victim doesn't blink. The witch doctor is powerless when his would-be accursed rejects the role of victim.

When hopelessness knocks, don't open the door and offer it a chair. Read hope-full literature. Choose to be around hope-full people. Memorize and feed on hope-full sentences. Listen to hope-full music.

As the movie *Hope Floats* concludes: "Beginnings are scary. Endings are usually sad. It's what's in the middle that counts. . . . Just give hope a chance to float up, and it will."

Use the space below to record your thoughts.

Chapter Nineteen

In the midst of winter, I finally learned there was within me an invincible summer.

Albert Camus

How long would you guess that a rat, put into a vat of water from which escape is impossible, can rat-paddle?

Curt Richter found out. He probably did more rat research than anyone in the twentieth century. In one experiment at Johns Hopkins Medical School, he studied stress by lowering wild Norway rats into big jars of water to see how long they could swim. If that was not enough stress for the poor rats, Richter squirted a jet of water into each container, agitating the water just enough to prevent the rat from floating and resting. The rats, on average, swam an unbelievable sixty hours before drowning!

A few rats, however, drowned almost instantly upon being introduced to the water. Richter was curious. He retraced his procedures and found a pattern. The few rats that drowned quickly had all been gripped in the researcher's hand, until they stopped fighting, before being placed into the water. Had they died of fright? Richter implanted electrodes in rats, repeated the experiment, and then conducted autopsies. He found that, while fear would have speeded up the heart and increased the blood pressure, these rats' hearts slowed down. They died with their hearts engorged with blood.

Richter's conclusion? They died a parasympathetic or submissive death. Restrained, they went passive. They gave up the struggle. What they did was the human equivalent of abandoning hope. In rats, and in humans, feeling helpless and hopeless can be lethal.

Then, Richter wondered, if these rats can be trained to lose hope, can we train them to have hope? He ran the experiment again. But this time, after restraining them and placing them into the water and watching them begin to go under, he performed a rescue—he plucked them out. Richter put them through the rescue routine several more times. They soon learned to paddle like crazy, expecting to escape.

Hopelessness is not just a bad habit—it is a lethal habit. Fortunately, it can be unlearned. Hope, like hopelessness, is a habit. Like riding a bicycle or speaking a foreign language, the more we practice it, the better we get at it. To hope, before we know it, can become second nature.

Use the space below to record your thoughts.

Chapter Twenty

I've been as terrified as the next person, but you
got to keep a-going; you've got to dream.
                                    Katharine Hepburn

A frog had lived on the banks of the Mississippi river
all his life. One day he decided to travel cross-
country to see what he could see, particularly to see how
frogs in other places fared. After several days' journey, he
came upon a frog that lived in a ditch in Arkansas. The
ditch was three feet deep and four feet wide.

The ditch frog, seeing company, saw opportunity to
impress. He jumped into the ditch, swam across it, hopped
out on the other side, and croaked to his guest, "Did you
see that? What did you think of that?" Then he swam back
across, showing off his backstroke. Unsure what the visi-
tor was thinking, the ditch frog asked him, "Tell me about
where you come from. What's it like? Is it like this?"

The Mississippi river frog simply replied, "You
wouldn't believe it if I told you. You would have to see for
yourself. Maybe someday I can take you there."

We, like the frog, live in a ditch. The name of our ditch is *here and now*. *Here* we can't see over the hill or around the bend. *Now* we are clueless as to what tomorrow will bring. Think of all the situations in your life from which you could see no exit, and there was one. Think of all the times it looked like the end of the world, and it wasn't. We learn, through our 20/20 "retrospectroscope," never to give up, because the future has possibilities impossible to see here and now, down in our ditch.

A cartoon celebrating Abraham Lincoln's birthday depicted two early-nineteenth-century settlers in Hodgenville, Kentucky, catching up on the local news. "Anything much going on in your neck of the woods?" one asked.

"Nothing much," said the other man. "Tom Lincoln's wife had another baby several days ago, but that's about it."

Use the space below to record your thoughts.

Chapter Twenty-One

A bird in the hand is a certainty, but a bird in the
bush may sing for you.

Bret Hart

Some are wishers, and some are hopers.

Wishers are passive. They "wish upon a star." They
wish that a genie or good fairy would miraculously appear
and grant their heart's desire. Wishers cross their fingers,
or sit on their hands, and wait. Wishers hunker down and
pray that a rescuer will come; that lightning—good luck—
will strike.

Hope, by contrast, is an active force. Martin Luther
King Jr. in his 1963 "I Have a Dream" speech used the
image of sculpting a "stone of hope" out of the mountain
of despair.

William Booth, spending a sleepless night in his comfortable London home, decided to go for a walk. He wandered into the poor sections of London and saw sights and
smelled odors he had never known were there. When he

arrived home, his wife Katherine, frantic over his disappearance, exclaimed, "Where on earth have you been?" William Booth said, "I've been to hell." Out of that eye-opening night, William and Katherine founded the Salvation Army.

Stan Curtis founded Kentucky Harvest. Observing restaurants throwing out large quantities of good leftovers, he began collecting the leftovers and giving them to the poor. Not content just to wish the hungry well, he sculpted out of the mountain of despair a stone of hope.

Sandra lost her firstborn son, Jared, to leukemia. Soon after his death she enrolled in nursing school. For the next quarter century she made relationships with sick and dying children her life's passion. She worked first as a nurse in a pediatric intensive-care unit, then as a pediatrics nurse for a hospice. She went beyond wishing others' little ones safety and health. Out of her mountain of despair she hewed a stone of hope.

Wishers wait. Hopers hew. Which am I? Which are you?

Use the space below to record your thoughts.

Chapter Twenty-Two

By your words you will be justified, and by your
words you will be condemned.

Matt. 12:37

Conducting a stress-reduction workshop for nurses, I
asked, "What sentences do you draw on when you're
having a bad day? What do you download from your brain
when someone says or does something that irritates you?"
The top three responses were:

1. *Consider the source.* "How stupid," one nurse said,
"to give away your peace of mind to someone you
may not even respect that much, to someone I
know is as flawed as I am."

2. *Choose your battles.* "You better learn the difference
between big stuff and little stuff, or you're in big
trouble. You've only got a finite amount of energy
and hours in a day, so you can't afford to squander
it. You can't fix everything, so you've got to put
first things first and let some things slide."

3. *This too shall pass.* "What we're going through now, we've been through before. We old-timers have lived through downsizing, cross-training, budget cutting, new leaders, centralization and decentralization, being bought and sold several times over. If you can flex and learn new things, you'll be fine."

What are your "go to" sentences? Whether you work in a hospital or a school, a factory or a department store, a fast-food restaurant or a government office, a home or a church, such sentences get you through the bad days. The programming in our central computer, the one housed in our skull—the thoughts we feed on, the way we talk to ourselves—keeps our hope alive. Or does us in.

Use the space below to record your thoughts.

Chapter Twenty-Three

Ever She Sought the Best, Ever She Found It.
(epitaph)

What kind of ancestor will you be? What epitaph is your life chiseling on your tombstone?

Reading epitaphs on tombstones is not as common an experience today as it once was. Back when the church was the epicenter of a community's social life, cemeteries were located next to the church. As people moved about the village, the cemetery next to the church offered a constant reality check, a reminder that all people, as Thomas Grey wrote, "await alike the inevitable hour—the paths of glory lead but to the grave."

I probably have spent more time in cemeteries than most. After reading Alex Haley's *Roots*, I stomped around many Tennessee cemeteries looking for my ancestors' tombstones. And as a hospital chaplain, I accompanied many families to their loved ones' final resting place.

As a lover of the Southwest, I've checked out many a picturesque "boot hill," reading inscriptions on tombstones and wondering how it must have been to have lived and died back then, out there. One epitaph on a tombstone outside a New Mexico village still inspires me. Under the name of a young woman who died in her twenties almost one hundred years ago, someone had chiseled these words: *Ever She Sought the Best, Ever She Found It.* At a time of no hospitals, no antibiotics, no modern conveniences—when one of every three babies didn't survive childhood—the verse this woman contributed to life's poem moved her ancestors to sum up her life: *Ever She Sought the Best, Ever She Found It.*

Some things, like human nature, never change. Still today, what we seek for is what we most likely find.

Some seek—and find—the worst. Some are working on an *Ever She Sought the Worst, Ever She Found It* tombstone inscription.

Jesus said, "Seek and you shall find." Hope is the way through life that ever seeks the best.

Use the space below to record your thoughts.

Chapter Twenty-Four

To travel hopefully is a better thing than to arrive.
Robert Louis Stevenson

Running low on hope? Had more than your share of setbacks? Come from a family of naysayers? Tend to put a negative spin on things? Suspect you were born under an unlucky star? Suffer from low self-esteem? Expect the worst?

The bad news is this: you probably will not metamorphosize one day into a hope-filled person.

The good news is this: hope, like any other habit or addiction, is cultivatable.

We came into the world hopeful, expecting to get our every craving (to be changed, fed, and held) satisfied. Between then and now we picked up some anti-hope thinking and anti-hope habits. Fortunately, anti-hope ways we may have learned can be unlearned.

Bob Wieland is a contemporary exemplar of hope. Several years back Bob crossed the finish line in the New York City Marathon, behind 19,412 racers. He ran the slowest time in the history of the marathon, requiring over four days to finish. Bob Wieland lost both his legs in Vietnam. For each "step," he had to use his arms like crutches to lift his torso and swing it forward. Bob had a statement to make at the end of the race: "The first step was the most difficult."

To grow hope, we have to take a hopeful step. We have to make ourselves act the way a hopeful person would act. We can't let it bother us that at first it doesn't feel quite right or that it's out of character or that it's not natural. Heart follows behavior. We have to make ourselves act the way we want to feel. Feelings have a way of catching up with behavior.

To grow some hope, take a hope-full step. That first step, Bob Wieland tells us, is the most difficult.

Use the space below to record your thoughts.

Chapter Twenty-Five

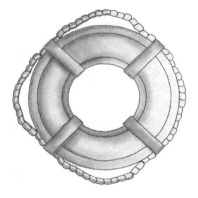

If you don't know where you're going, you'll end
up somewhere else.

Yogi Berra

Do you know where you're going?

In the film *City Slickers*, Jack Palance plays Curly, a crusty
but contented old cowboy whose life is leading cattle drives.
One day Curly glanced over at the three dudes from back East
who had joined him for two weeks of "finding themselves."
With a wise, knowing smile, he held up his forefinger.

City slicker: "What in the world does that mean?"

    Curly: "One thing."

City slicker: "But what is the one thing?"

    Curly: "That's for you to find out."

To be clear on who we are—on what moves us, what
stirs our passions, what makes meaning out of our life—is
to know, with Curly, our "one thing."

Louis Pasteur made his life work one thing. In a time when tens of thousands died every year from rabies, Pasteur worked tirelessly to develop a rabies vaccine. When nine-year-old Joseph Meister was severely bitten by a rabid dog, Joseph's mother begged and finally persuaded Pasteur to experiment on her son. Pasteur injected Joseph Meister for ten days. The boy lived. Pasteur found that accomplishment so sweet that he asked for only three words to make it to his tombstone: "Joseph Meister Lived!"

Abraham Jacobi made his life work one thing. No one, since Pasteur found a way to get germs out of milk, did more for pediatrics than Jacobi. Before Jacobi, pediatrics was a sub-specialty under gynecology. "The Dean of Pediatrics," Jacobi died in his eighties, but not before exacting from his family a promise that only two words would appear on his grave marker: "I Served."

Embroiled as we are in many things, we need periodically to step back and ask ourselves whether we are being true to our one thing. All that counts, Curly might say, is to keep the main thing, the main thing.

Use the space below to record your thoughts.

Chapter Twenty-Six

No pessimist ever discovered the secrets of the
stars, or sailed to an enchanted land, or opened a
new doorway to the human spirit.

Helen Keller

How do we understand the spirit of a person like
Helen Keller, who, against all odds, presses on and
prevails?

Born healthy, at the age of nineteen months Helen
came down with a fever that left her permanently unable
to see, hear, or speak. Despite the enormity of her handi-
cap, in her twenties she became the first deaf and blind
person ever to graduate cum laude from college. She
completed her degree at Radcliffe in only four years. Deaf
and blind, she graduated proficient in Greek, Latin,
French, and German.

Helen Keller became a tireless spokesperson for
women's right to vote, for working people to strike,
against capital punishment, and against the use of nuclear
weapons. By the time of her death at age eighty-eight,

Helen Keller had become a role model for millions of little girls and an inspiration for disabled people everywhere.

Hope isn't really hope so long as it remains a nice, fair-weather ideal. Hope that hasn't been put to the test isn't real hope—it is a sweet, lofty principle held in a vacuum. How is it that those who have obstacle-strewn lives, who have suffered most, who have had their hope tested most, sometimes evolve into the world's most positive, inspirational people?

Two forces converged powerfully in Helen Keller's life, and they largely account for her place in our hearts. One was the intervention, when Helen was seven years old, of a private teacher named Anne Sullivan. Having lost her own sight at age five, Anne Sullivan was sent to a poor-house when her family broke up. Out of that education in adversity she brought a deep reservoir of empathy, compassion, and patience to the task of reaching and teaching Helen Keller. Through Anne Sullivan's intervention, Helen came to believe, as she later wrote: "Although the world is full of suffering, it is also full of the overcoming of it." Would we ever have heard of Helen Keller if Anne Sullivan had not befriended and motivated her?

One force—the relationship with Anne Sullivan—came from without. The other came from within. The inner force was Helen Keller's irrepressible, iron will. In mid-life she wrote, "Life is either a daring adventure or it is nothing." Late in life, asked about growing older, she said, "All my life I have tried to avoid ruts, such as doing things my ancestors did before me, or leaning on the crutches of other people's opinions, or losing my childhood sense of wonderment."

Could this be life's most powerful one-two combination—having a friend who truly believes in us, plus having a dogged determination to avoid ruts and keep a childlike sense of wonderment? Is this the recipe for making life a daring, hope-filled adventure?

Perhaps there are other disheartened Helen Kellers out there. We may become for them the Anne Sullivan who helps them "sail to an enchanted land."

Use the space below to record your thoughts.

Chapter Twenty-Seven

Each of us must ask ourselves one question: What
am I doing to increase the sum of hope in this world?
Arthur Burns

What is life's most important question? What are
the answers humans most often give to this question? The ten top contenders are:

1. Who are your parents?
2. How many children and grandchildren did you have?
3. How high did you rise in the company?
4. How many people reported to you?
5. What was your net worth?
6. What organizations claimed you as a member?
7. How many degrees did you have after your name?
8. What religion are you?
9. How many years did you live?
10. How long was your obituary?

Psychiatrist Karl Menninger rejected all of the above as
life's most important question and offered this substitute:

"What are you doing to help dilute the misery in the world?" If that sounds a little negative, hear economist Arthur Burns's more positive rendition of that philosophy. He gave this charge to a commencement crowd at Hebrew University in Jerusalem: "Each of us must ask ourselves one question: What am I doing to increase the sum of hope in this world?"

That's why many choose to work in hospitals! People come in sick and go home well. Or, we trust, if not well, at least well cared for. Call it "diluting misery" or call it "increasing the sum of hope in the world" or call it simply "service." Whatever it is called, is there any higher, nobler, more satisfying use of a life?

Whether we find it in a soup kitchen, a homeless shelter, a scout troop, a hospice, Meals on Wheels, Habitat for Humanity, a nursing home, a church, a classroom, or a hospital room, there's plenty of misery out there to go around. The most contented people may be those who look it in the eye and work to dilute it.

Use the space below to record your thoughts.

Twenty-Eight

Hope is the thing with feathers that perches in the soul, that sings the song without the words and never stops at all.

Emily Dickinson

Tom is an optimist. He studies the evidence. Out of his research he makes a case for the stock market to finish the year up, or that people are basically good, or that he will live to be one hundred.

Dick lives in denial. He turns a deaf ear to hints from his wife that their marriage is in trouble. He doesn't listen to his physician who warns him to give up fast food or he'll destroy his heart.

Harry hopes. He acknowledges that his prognosis is bad and that the odds are overwhelmingly against him. Nevertheless, he chooses to go with the long-shot possibility that there's a cure somewhere out there, instead of accepting the odds.

Hope. Denial. Optimism. We should not confuse hope with the other two. Denial refuses to face facts. Optimism builds a credible case—from the facts—for a good out-come. Hope is different. Hope can admit that the odds are terrible, that it's impossible—based on the facts—to be optimistic. Nevertheless, hope chooses to cast its lot, not with the negative probabilities, but with a good (however improbable) possibility.

Hope is always a rational option, even for the dying person. The dying person, who may have given up all hope for a cure, still hopes to have friendly faces at the bedside to the end, and medication adequate for the pain.

Hope—living or dying—is the thing. Always.

Use the space below to record your thoughts.

Twenty-Nine

I was a stranger, and you welcomed me.

Jesus

M eet Anne MacMeans Jamison, pioneer woman. She longs to teach us something about strangers.

When the Revolutionary War broke out, Anne, her husband, and their seven children headed west. Leaving Pennsylvania, they floated down the Ohio River and stayed for a year at a little settlement in Kentucky near what would later be named Louisville. But because of a land dispute, they moved farther down the river to the confluence of the Ohio and Mississippi rivers, near present-day Paducah. With a few other settlers, they built a fort, cleared the land, and planted corn.

One night, in early summer of 1780, Native Americans attacked the fort, killing four of the men and taking one other prisoner. All of the corn was cut down. Faced with slaughter or starvation, nineteen survivors, "having got enough of our new settlements," boarded their boats and floated south, hoping to reach Natchez, three hundred miles away.

One by one, the wilderness wanderers died of malaria or starvation. Anne's husband died first. Two of their children died. Then one day, just when two surviving adults had agreed all hope was lost—a stranger appeared on the shore. "He had killed a bear," Anne later wrote in her memoirs, "and had followed us in [his] canoe with kind intentions." He gave the starving Caucasians a quarter of the bear and some dried venison, and disappeared into the forest. His gift saved their lives. Anne later wrote, "Those who live in plenty, fed to full, cannot readily conceive how precious the gift of food is, even if sent by the hand of a Savage, who is more likely to murder than relieve us."

Anne and five of her children made it to Natchez. Anne wrote in her journal, "We were truly in a deplorable condition and had little probability of recovering. Strangers did everything in their power for our recovery."

Anne, who was forty years of age at the time, lived into her eighties. Near the end of her memoirs, thinking back to the "Savage" on the shore and to the strangers at Natchez who nurtured her and her children back to health, she laid an onus on her readers: "May none of mine, nor any who reads this narrative, ever deal harshly with a stranger."

How many times in our lives do strangers—with nothing to gain, without mercenary motives, maybe at considerable cost to themselves, maybe never to cross our path again—come to our aid?

How sweet it is occasionally to *be* the stranger, to make a meteoric appearance in the life of some Anne MacMeans Jamison, bestow a blessing, and exit the stage.

Take a few minutes to reflect on what you've just read.

Chapter Thirty

> Hope, till hope creates from its own wreck the thing it anticipates.
>
> Percy Bysshe Shelley

Why does hope come so hard for some of us? Is it genetic—we're born with it or we're not—or is hope a habit we learn?

Animal studies suggest that hope and hopelessness are largely habits that are learned.

Walleyed pike, in one experiment, were placed in a tank of water and fed all the minnows they could hold. One day a thick glass was placed between the pike and the minnows. The pike banged up against the glass time and again, going after the minnows. Eventually they quit trying. When the researchers removed the glass, the pike made no further attempt to eat the minnows. The pike all starved to death, their favorite dinner swimming circles around them. The pike had learned hopelessness.

In another study, dogs were placed in boxes and administered mild shocks. The dogs tried to escape, but there was no way out. Soon they quit trying. The next day the doors on the boxes were adjusted so that the dogs could easily escape. Most of the dogs made no attempt to leave. When they were shocked, they laid in their boxes and whimpered. They had learned hopelessness.

It's hard, when doors get slammed in our faces or on our toes a few times, to keep going back to the door. That's what makes hope so precious. It's a habit that defiantly, hoping-against-hope, refuses to quit. Representing the hopeful spirit, Emily Dickinson wrote, "O Jesus in the air, I know not which Thy chamber is. I'm knocking every-where."

Use the space below to record your thoughts.

Chapter Thirty-One

We live in the shadowlands. The sun is always shining somewhere else—around a bend in the road, over the brow of a hill.

C. S. Lewis

Here in the shadowlands, it is sometimes hard to find our way. We don't see things clearly or objectively. And it's impossible to foresee how drastically things may change tomorrow. "Now we see through a glass darkly," the Bible says.

In 1783, president Ezra Stiles of Yale, living in the shadowlands, predicted that the American religious landscape of the future would be equally divided between Congregationalists, Episcopalians, and Presbyterians (the three leading denominations in colonial America). At about the same time, Thomas Jefferson, living in the shadowlands, predicted that in a few years all Americans would be Unitarians.

In 1901, the Daimler-Benz company, working in the shadowlands, announced that the number of horseless carriages would never exceed one million because it would not be possible to train enough chauffeurs.

We can't see the future any more clearly than could our illustrious foremothers and forefathers. Was there one seer on the planet in 1970 who imagined in his or her wildest dreams that the North Atlantic Treaty Organization, formed to defend its member countries against arch-enemy Russia, would in 2002 invite Russia to join them as a member?

When we can't see how any good can possibly come out of a situation, when we can't see a way of escape, maybe we should take a deep breath and remind ourselves that it has to be that way, living here in the shadowlands. Paths do open. But it is impossible in our present darkness to see them.

Use the space below to record your thoughts.

Chapter Thirty-Two

> We are all standing in the mud, but we can still look at the stars.
>
> Reg Green

The mud in which we're stuck may, unfortunately, be permanent. Like a birth defect. Or a chronic illness. Or infertility. Or a chemical addiction. Or the death of a child.

The mud in which we're stuck may, fortunately, be a condition that, with time and opportunity and the will of the stuck one, can pass. Like unemployment. Or hunger. Or morbid obesity. Or homelessness.

Reg and Maggie Green suffered what most would agree is life's greatest tragedy. In September 1994, while Reg and Maggie and their two children were vacationing in southern Italy, robbers, in a botched car-jacking, shot out the windows of their rental car. Nicholas, age seven, was asleep in the back seat. A bullet struck him in the head.

Nicholas was rushed to the hospital and placed on life support. In a little over a day's time it was determined that

Nicholas was brain dead. His parents consented to organ donation. His heart, both kidneys, both corneas, his liver, and his pancreas went to seven Italians.

In the following year, requests for organ donation cards quadrupled in Italy, and organ donations doubled. The rise in donations came to be called "the Nicholas effect." The magnanimity of Nicholas's parents inspired others to give.

When asked how they could have the presence of mind and the compassion to donate Nicholas's organs, Reg Green said: "I keep coming back to a truth I learned long ago: we are all standing in the mud, but we can still look at the stars."

Lift up your eyes!

Use the space below to record your thoughts.

Chapter Thirty-Three

> Nothing is impossible. Sometimes I have believed
> as many as six impossible things before breakfast.
> Lewis Carroll, *Alice in Wonderland*

The life of David Ben-Gurion, born David Gruen in
Poland, defines "hard-core realist." He moved to
what is now the state of Israel in 1906 and helped create
the first agricultural workers' commune, the forerunner of
the highly successful kibbutz movement. During World
War II he helped save European Jewry and inspired many
Jews to join the British forces and fight the Nazis. He led
the struggle to establish the state of Israel in 1948 and
facilitated the ingathering of Jewish exiles from the four
corners of the earth. Modern Israel considers him one of
history's great revolutionaries, in the tradition of Moses
and George Washington.

Philosopher and historian Sidney Hook terms
Judaism's modern King David an "event-making man."
"Eventful" people, by contrast, are those who are thrust

into historical events and turn out to be right for the time, Hook says. But David Ben-Gurion, Israel's first and longest-serving prime minister, was an "event-making man"—one of those rare individuals who drive history in the direction they chart. Of the survival of the Jews and the improbable establishment of the state of Israel, David Ben-Gurion commented, "In Israel, in order to be a realist, you must believe in miracles."

If "miracle" is defined as an improbable, surprising, joyful, inexplicable event or turn of events—do you believe in miracles? Have you ever seen one?

I once asked some hospital staff: "Have you ever experienced a miracle?" One man told of the day when he was at the end of his rope, broke, not knowing where his next meal would come from—and someone slipped an envelope under his front door that contained $16. He never knew who did that. Another man told of a time he was totally discouraged in his job, burned out, embittered, ready to quit—and someone left a message from a Chinese fortune cookie on his desk that read: "There are good possibilities that you have not yet seen." That message was the tonic that helped his spirit U-turn. Another told of a Christmas when he and his wife couldn't afford Christmas gifts, even for each other. They could not afford even a Christmas tree—but several days before Christmas there appeared on their front porch a little artificial Christmas tree. They still have no idea who put it there, but they still have the tree—their little "Christmas miracle."

Whether on a global or individual scale, unbelievably good things are happening. Sometimes, like David Ben-Gurion, we can help make it happen. Sometimes, thank goodness, we're on the receiving end of an unearned, unexpected gift—pure, wonderful, amazing grace.

And sometimes we have the opportunity to become, for someone else, the miracle-maker.

Use the space below to record your thoughts.

Chapter Thirty-Four

Ever tried? Ever failed? No matter. Try again. Fail again. Fail better.

Samuel Beckett

In the closing decades of the twentieth century, my wife and I reared three sons. We are grateful for several heroic figures Hollywood served up for their inspiration and emulation in their formative years.

First came *Star Wars*, with Han Solo and Luke Skywalker battling Darth Vader and the evil empire. For years our house featured a model of the Millennium Falcon and figures of Chewbacca and Obi-won Kenobi, Yoda and C3PO, droids and Ewoks. In our kitchen we still have an R2-D2 ice bucket. The message of *Star Wars* for children—evil is real; be one of the good guys.

Then in 1976 came *Rocky*. Rocky Balboa, not the biggest or strongest or fastest or smartest boxer, kept coming back, kept getting up when knocked down, never gave up, and ultimately went the distance and prevailed. My wife and I cried when we first saw the movie in Philadelphia in 1976.

One of our sons, a championship runner in high school, played the theme song from *Rocky* before each big race.

Rudy, in 1992, enacted the true story of Rudy Ruettiger. As a child, small and unathletic, Rudy dreamed of playing football for the Fighting Irish of Notre Dame. In his early twenties, when his best friend died in a work accident, Rudy decided it was time to pursue his dream. First he enrolled in a junior college in South Bend. Then he got a job working as a groundskeeper at Knute Rockne Stadium. Next he got accepted into Notre Dame as a student. Finally he landed a spot on the scout team. In the last minutes of Notre Dame's final home game, the coach sent Rudy into the game. He tackled the quarterback! His teammates carried him off the field on their shoulders. The take-home message for children (and adults as well): forgo instant gratification; tenaciously follow your dream.

I like the way Martin Luther admonished his colleague Melancthon to fight the good fight: "Be a sinner and sin boldly, but believe and rejoice in grace even more boldly." Instead of advocating sin with his "sin boldly" wording, Luther meant something like what Beckett meant by "Fail again. Fail better." The message: Timidity is a sin. Don't be so afraid of messing up that you do nothing. Live boldly. Take risks. This philosophy holds true especially for Christians, who believe that God's grace covers our failures.

There's a war going on out there. It's a spiritual war between good and evil, hope and fear, boldness and timidity, life and death. Don't shrink back. Choose life!

Take a few minutes to reflect on what you've just read.

Chapter Thirty-Five

The only thing we have to fear is fear itself.
Franklin D. Roosevelt

There's an old Egyptian story about a little boy named Miobi who came to a village where the people were very strange. They did little more than moan and groan about almost everything. The fires didn't get lit, the goats didn't get milked, the children didn't get clothed, and the crops didn't get planted, all because the villagers were expecting any time to get eaten by the monster that lived on top of the mountain.

Miobi looked up, and behold—the monster was real. He had a head like a crocodile and a body like a hippopotamus and a tail like a very fat snake. Smoke and fire came from his nostrils. The villagers lived in dread that any day the monster might come down and devour them.

Miobi said to the villagers, "I will go up the mountain by myself and challenge the monster." The villagers pleaded with him not to go, sure that he would never return. Miobi began to climb the mountain, and as he climbed higher and higher and got nearer and nearer, the monster looked smaller and smaller. "This is a very curious phenomenon indeed," thought Miobi. "When I run away from the monster, the monster gets larger, but the nearer I get to it, the smaller it becomes."

When at last Miobi reached the cave, instead of a gigantic monster, he found a quiet little creature about the size of a toad. It purred. Miobi picked it up and put it in his pocket and headed back down the mountain.

When the villagers saw Miobi safe and sound, they wanted to make him their god for slaying the monster. Miobi explained exactly what had happened and how he had brought the "monster" back down the mountain as a pet. He showed them the little toad-like creature. "What is your name?" the villagers asked. The monster answered, "I have many names. Some call me famine, and some pestilence; some call me war, and some cancer." Then the little creature yawned and added, "But most people call me What Might Happen."

The message is a simple one: Don't be controlled by What Might Happen.

Use the space below to record your thoughts.

Chapter Thirty-Six

The lowest ebb is the turn of the tide.
Henry Wadsworth Longfellow

At age sixteen, Reggie served time for the first time—a seven-month stint in reform school. He joined the military at age eighteen and promptly earned a dishonorable discharge. Eleven of his next thirteen years were spent in prison, all for petty crimes. He married three times in those years and lost track of how many children he fathered by those three and other women.

Reggie convinced himself at age thirty-three that he was too smart for a life of petty crime. It was time for him to move up to the next level—to go big time. He decided that he should rob a bank, a really big bank. He went to a department store and bought a red ski mask. He folded a paper sack and put it in his coat pocket. He wrote a note in big, legible letters: THIS IS A STICKUP. PUT ALL YOUR MONEY IN THIS BAG. DON'T SET OFF ANY ALARMS. He got his gun and drove off to the bank. He parked the car, took a deep breath, got out of his car, and walked to the bank door. It was locked. There was a sign on the door: *Closed for Memorial Day*. Foiled again!

Cursing under and over his breath, Reggie started home. Flashing blue lights appeared in his rearview mirror. Reggie was driving 44 in a 35-mph zone. When the police officer walked up to his car and looked in, he saw the ski mask and gun and sack and note, all lying very orderly on the front seat. Reggie was sent back to prison.

There's a happy ending to this true story. At one point Reggie accepted help from some good people who wanted to save him from a pathetic life. Today he is happily married and happily employed, and is proud to have taken no sick days in three years. Today Reggie is your rock-solid citizen. When he was at the end of his rope, he reached out to Alcoholics Anonymous, and they took him in.

Although there are exceptions to the rule, many alcoholics who achieve sobriety through Alcoholics Anonymous believe that those addicted to alcohol unfortunately have to "hit rock bottom"—lose their spouse, children, job, everything—before they're seriously ready to reform.

The good news is that even when we've hit rock bottom and lost it all—like Reggie—there's still hope!

Two truths from the physical world support this fundamental truth about human nature. One, the lowest ebb is truly the turn of the tide. And two, only when it's dark enough can we see the stars.

Take a few minutes to reflect on what you've just read.

Chapter Thirty-Seven

You don't get to choose how you're going to die
or when. You can only decide how you're going
to live.

Joan Baez

Probably no society on earth appreciates the wisdom
of its elders less than Americans. Native Americans,
people in the Far East and Middle East, and African cul-
tures listen reverently to their wise old tribal elders for
guidance, while in America we worship youth.

For four Sundays in October, several years ago, mem-
bers of the Seekers Sunday school class that I taught sat at
the feet of sixteen of the church's matriarchs and patri-
archs. Each Sunday four got their ten minutes of fame—
ten minutes to sit and speak, *ex cathedra*, on the topic
"What I Have Learned." Here was their assignment:
"Reflect back over your life experience and then share
with us two of the most valuable pieces of wisdom you've
acquired, the things you deem most worthy of passing

along to the next generation. You have ten minutes." What they gave us was, more than any credit card, priceless.

One woman named Carrie gave us this simple truth she wanted to pass on: "The most important thing I've learned," she said, "is that you choose to be happy." She explained how her father had always been a happy person. She told how, one time when he was carrying a tray of cafeteria food to the table, he tripped and spilled part of his drink. His comment to the family as he looked at his half-filled glass and smiled was, "Thank goodness I didn't want any more to drink than that!"

Her mother, Carrie said, by contrast had always been an unhappy person. Several weeks earlier, when she had gone to visit her mother in the nursing home, Carrie said, "Mom, I'm going to take you out to eat and then we'll do some shopping." In the car on the way to shop, Carrie noticed that her mother was crying. She asked, "Mother, what's wrong?" Her mother said, "This time tomorrow it will all be over and I won't have anything to look forward to." Carrie's conclusion: "Happiness is a choice. I decided as a child that I would be like my father and have a happy life."

Holding a hopeful worldview is a two-part process. First comes *Decision* with a capital D—the philosophical and theological choice we make at some point for happiness over unhappiness, gratitude over ingratitude, joy and celebration over doom and gloom.

Then there's *decision* with a lowercase d, which may be the more difficult of the two. We make that one every morning when we crawl out of bed—whether to behave this one day as one who has said Yes to life.

Take a few minutes to reflect on what you've just read.

Chapter Thirty-Eight

When I was ten years old, I had the dream of being the best in the world at something.

Arnold Schwarzenegger

L ook around. So much of nature appears to have a built-in purpose, an end toward which it is moving. An acorn is pregnant, not with a cornstalk or dogwood or pumpkin, but an oak. A human zygote yearns to become an embryo, the embryo to become a fetus, the fetus to become a newborn baby, the baby to become an adult. There seems to be a magnetic force in nature drawing each entity, as true north draws the compass, toward its unique destiny.

Could this be true of every individual human being? Carl Jung wrote, "In the final analysis, we count for something only because of the essential we embody, and if we do not embody that, life is wasted." The Greeks called this "essential we embody" our *daimon*. Our *daimon* is the carrier of our destiny. It wants us to evolve fully into our ideal self.

Some of us have a keen sense, either of generally carrying greatness within us, or of the specific *daimon* we carry. Sigmund Freud, from his very early years, felt absolutely certain that he would achieve something monumental with his life, as did his family, who organized their whole life around Sigmund's evolution. Golda Meir, prime minister of Israel (1969–1974), in the fourth grade organized a school protest movement against a required purchase of textbooks that were too expensive for the poor children to buy. She rented out a hall to hold a fundraising meeting and addressed the meeting, much as she would later lead her country through war. Carl Sagan considered high school a waste of his time, but he graduated valedictorian and his classmates voted him "Most Likely to Succeed." A rhyme accompanied his yearbook picture: "Astronomy research is Carl's main aim; an excellent student, he should achieve fame." One of the freshman students who lived on the same dormitory floor said of Sagan's room full of science fiction books, "We'd all read science fiction and gotten over it. This was the room of someone who hadn't."

Rabbi Zusya wrote, "In the next life I will not be asked, 'Why were you not Moses?' I will be asked, 'Why were you not Zusya?'"

You can be the very best in all the world, in all of history, at one thing—being you.

How does your acorn grow?

Take a few minutes to reflect on what you've just read.

Chapter Thirty-Nine

I know the plans I have for you, says the LORD,
plans for your welfare and not for harm, to give
you a future with hope.

Jer. 29:11

In the Judeo-Christian tradition, hope is not primarily a psychological construct. Hope in the Bible is not optimism or positive thinking or "accentuating the positive." Hope derives its meaning from a faithful God who goes before and invites, "Come follow me"; a God who promises believers a good future.

Anne Lamott discovered, or was discovered by, this God of hope. Anne grew up a bit of a "flower child," surrounded by booze and pot and unbelief. She virtually memorized at an early age Bertrand Russell's essay: "Why I Am Not a Christian." "None of the adults in our circle believed," she wrote. "Believing meant that you were stupid. Ignorant people believed, uncouth people believed, and we were heavily couth."

After years of promiscuity, cocaine, psychedelic mushrooms, and alcohol abuse, destructive relationships, pregnancies, an abortion, and suicidal thinking, one day she wandered—very hungover—past a ramshackle Presbyterian church in a poor neighborhood. The music she heard coming from inside the church spoke to her. She found herself going back about once a month, standing outside and listening to the music. One day she went inside and listened. She later wrote that the music "pulled me in and split me open."

Anne never stayed for the sermon, because she didn't want to be preached to. But then one Sunday she decided to stay. The minister told a story about a little girl who got lost and couldn't find her way home. A policeman drove her around until she recognized her church, and the little girl told the policeman, "You can let me out now. That's my church, and I can always find my way home from here." Anne joined that church. Today she's an elder. Of her church, to which she dedicated her best-selling book *Traveling Mercies*, she wrote, "No matter how bad I am feeling, how lost or lonely or frightened, when I see the faces of the people at my church, and hear their tawny voices, I can always find my way home."

Enoch, an Amish boy, decided at age sixteen to leave the family compound and strike out on his own. The turning point in Enoch's spiritual journey was a dream. Having struggled inwardly for several years over whether to remain Amish or incur the rejection of his family by leaving, he experienced a dream that helped him make up his mind. In the dream, the sky was filled with rainbows. Enoch saw a man sealing off a big hole in the ground with mortar and stone. Enoch looked into the hole, and it looked like it went down forever. Enoch asked the man, "If I fall in there, how far will I go?" The man answered,

"Not far, because I will catch you." That dream gave Enoch the courage to leave home, like Abraham of old leaving Ur, not knowing where he was going. When my faith wavers, I sometimes think of Enoch and his sky of rainbows and the mysterious man's promise to catch him should he fall.

God is faithful, and wants us to have a future and a hope.

Use the space below to record your thoughts.

Chapter Forty

Despair is never an answer; despair is a question.
Elie Weisel

Years ago I came to know quite well a single mother
who had one son, Sam, who was the darling of his
mother's eye. Sam was a star pitcher for several seasons on
his Little League team. One day he was diagnosed with
cancer. A bone marrow transplant failed, and Sam died.

Sam's mother is an active church member. Several years
after Sam died the church organized a drive to purchase
new hymnals for the sanctuary, and she bought several in
memory of Sam. Because of her generosity, and the loss of
her son, the church elders invited her to pray the main
prayer on the day the hymnals were dedicated. Here is her
prayer:

> Dear God. It's been a long time since I spoke to
> you—about five years, I think, so you may not
> remember my voice. I am here to offer a prayer of
> dedication. I have no words of praise or thanksgiving

for you for the death of children. For this, I have only silent words of rage. I have no words of praise or thanksgiving for you for the destruction that results in the lives of parents and friends when their broken bodies stop struggling and are finally consumed in the fire of death. For this I have only silent words of rage. I have no words of praise or thanksgiving for you for rampant evil and suffering in your creation so pervasive and intense that it is far beyond our ability to endure. For this there are no words—only silence. Yet, amidst wreckage and despair, there remain three tiny words of praise and thanksgiving. For the exquisite beauty of my child Sam, I offer you words of praise and thanksgiving now and forever. For motherhood. For allowing me the high privilege of being a mother, and the higher privilege of being Sam's mother, I offer you words of praise and thanksgiving now and forever. . . . Three words of silence, three words of praise I offer you from the broken remains of a mother's heart. Of all present here, only you and I know how pitiful an offering it really is.

Sam's mother composed that prayer, but she couldn't deliver it. She added this postscript to the copy she gave me:

I huddled in the last pew, in the back, in the corner. How could I praise God? God had refused my offering of a faithful, living child, apparently preferring the charred and brutalized remains of a dead sacrifice. I wonder what I did to merit outer darkness?

Many years have passed now. Sam's mother continues to struggle, protest, rage, remember, grieve, and fight depression. She took her quest for meaning to seminary and then into the ministry. For some, like her, question-ing is the peculiar form hope takes. It's their alternative to a descent into outer darkness.

Use the space below to record your thoughts.

Chapter Forty-One

Life is a petty thing unless it is moved by the indomitable urge to extend its boundaries.

José Ortega y Gasset

Maya Angelou mentions in many of her lectures that she is trying to be a Christian. She says she is amazed when people come up to her and introduce themselves with the words "I am a Christian." She is always tempted to reply, and sometimes does, "Already? You've got it already?"

Is the life of faith a status, or a quest? Is it more an achievement, or a journey; more a location, or a path; something we have attained, or something we're working on?

I find Erich Fromm's distribution of personality types into "necrophilous" and "biophilous" useful. Necrophilous, from the Greek *nekros*, "death," describes that aspect of us that loves to keep things frozen, fixed, machine-like, orderly, and therefore controllable. Ada Petrova and Peter Watson studied newly released documents on Adolf Hitler and made this observation: "All his habits—the clothes he wore till they disintegrated, his toothbrushing routines, the music and movies he selected, his time schedules—were repetitive. When he took his dog for a walk, which he did every day at the same time, he threw the same piece of wood from exactly the same spot in the same direction." Sameness is sacred to the necrophilous (death-loving) personality. Change is the enemy.

Biophilous, from the Greek *bio*, "life," describes that part of us that embraces life—our open, receptive, adventurous, spontaneous, fun-loving self; the dimension of us given to growing and improving.

Christianity's greatest change-agent in the last thousand years was Martin Luther. "This life," Luther wrote, "is not godliness but the process of becoming godly, not health but getting well, not being but becoming, not rest but exercise. We are not now what we shall be, but we are on the way. The process is not yet finished, but it is actively going on. This is not the goal, but it is the right road. At present, everything does not gleam and sparkle, but everything is being cleansed."

Death-loving or life-loving? Give in to that indomitable urge to expand your boundaries!

Use the space below to record your thoughts.

Chapter Forty-Two

The ability to rise is the nobleness of the human spirit.

Maya Angelou

Once on a trip to Texarkana for a speaking engagement, I exited the interstate at Hope and drove thirty miles south to Stamps, Arkansas. I wanted to see where Maya Angelou grew up. I came away with a more profound appreciation of this woman's improbable rise from dire poverty and abuse to write *I Know Why the Caged Bird Sings*; the majestic poem she wrote for the first Clinton inauguration, *On the Pulse of Morning*; and my favorite, *And Still I Rise*. Her evolution from the lowliest of beginnings in Stamps, Arkansas, epitomizes the nobility of the human spirit—the ability to rise!

One of America's holidays celebrates the human spirit's noble ability to rise. When the Pilgrims sat down to the first Thanksgiving in 1621, half their family and friends had perished, either on the voyage over or in the New World. William Bradford, their governor for thirty-five years, wrote, "That which was most sad and lamentable was that in two or three months' time, especially in January and February, being the depth of winter, and wanting houses and other comforts; being infected with the scurvy and other diseases . . . there died sometimes two or three a day."

So what did the Pilgrims do? They rose to hold a Thanksgiving service. Bradford prayed that a better day would come when their children would rise up and praise them and say, "Our fathers were Englishmen who came over this great ocean and were ready to perish in the wilderness; but they cried unto the Lord, and He heard their voice and looked on their adversity. Let them therefore, praise the Lord because He is good and His mercies endure forever."

When Abraham Lincoln proclaimed the first national day of Thanksgiving, he did so in the wake of the battle of Shiloh, where a total of 25,000 Union and Confederate troops died, in the midst of a war that would claim over half a million lives (2 percent of the new nation's population). Twice as many more died of disease and starvation and other causes. So what did Lincoln do? He rose to proclaim a day, not of doom and gloom and grief, but a day of Thanksgiving.

The quality is not American, but human. It is the noblest aspect of our humanity—the ability, like dust or air or Maya Angelou, to rise.

Take a few minutes to reflect on what you've just read.

Chapter Forty-Three

In every winter heart there is a quivering spring.
Kahlil Gibran

On Christmas Day, 1863, America's foremost poet sat broken and forlorn.

Henry Wadsworth Longfellow was well born, having John and Priscila Alden in his American pedigree and a prominent New England lawyer for a father. Henry was a precocious boy, reading classical literature at age six, and graduating from college and becoming a professor of modern language before his twentieth birthday.

A little over a year after he married and moved to Boston to teach at Harvard, his wife became ill and died. He didn't remarry for seven years. He and his second wife had five children. It was in this time of his life that Longfellow wrote most of his famous poems, poems that made him wealthy and famous worldwide. But tragedy struck again in 1861 when his second wife, lighting a match, accidentally set her dress on fire and burned to death.

The Civil War exacerbated Longfellow's grief. He hated war and hated slavery. In the early days of the war, his oldest son, nineteen-year-old Charles, was critically wounded and paralyzed in battle.

On Christmas Day, 1863, as Longfellow listened to the ringing of the church bells, the madness of war and the remoteness of peace overwhelmed him. He took up his pen. The opening verses of *I Heard the Bells on Christmas Day* are heavy and dark, somber and hopeless. In verse three the cynicism peaks: "And in despair I bowed my head. 'There is no peace on earth,' I said. 'For hate is strong and mocks the song of peace on earth, goodwill to men.'"

The composition, straight from his grief-stricken heart, would never have become one of the world's most popular Christmas carols had he not finished on an unmistakable note of hope in verse six: "Then pealed the bells more loud and deep: 'God is not dead, nor doth He sleep; The wrong shall fail, the right prevail, with peace on earth, goodwill to men."

Sometimes it takes some *thing* to connect us to the hope within us, especially in a time of *extremis*, like idiotic war or personal bereavement. A symbol may help transport us there. A sunrise. A rainbow. A crocus. A cross. Or the ringing of church bells on Christmas Day.

Use the space below to record your thoughts.

Chapter Forty-Four

The only difference between saints and sinners is that every saint has a past while every sinner has a future.

Oscar Wilde

I f ever there was a lost cause, it was old Ebenezer Scrooge. Who was Scrooge? According to Charles Dickens, "Oh! But he was a tight-fisted hand at the grindstone. Scrooge! a squeezing, wrenching, grasping, scraping, clutching, covetous old sinner. . . . He carried his own low temperature always around with him. . . . No warmth could warm, nor wintry weather chill him. No wind that blew was bitterer than he."

Dickens, writing *A Christmas Carol* at the time of the Industrial Revolution, knew firsthand the great disparity between industrial exploiters and industrial exploitees. As a child, the second of eight children, he had worked in a boot-blacking factory, while his daddy (who couldn't pay his debts) was in a debtors' prison, along with the rest of the Dickens family. Christmas represented, for Charles

Dickens, a break, a time-out from all that. Christmas was humankind's best effort to bridge the gap between the haves and the have-nots, or, in Dickens's words, "the only time in the long calendar of the year when men and women seem by one consent to open their shut-up hearts freely, and to think of other people below them as if they really were fellow-passengers to the grave, and not another race of creatures bound on other journeys."

On Christmas Eve, having met others' "Merry Christmas" all day with a "Bah, Humbug," Scrooge retired to his office to count the money he has made fleecing the poor, when a series of ghosts helped Scrooge see his money-grubbing life for what it was. The Ghost of Christmas Yet to Come ultimately got through to the old coot, permitting Scrooge to foresee his own death, to overhear people discussing his death and dismissing it lightly, to watch people fighting over his belongings, even down to the sheets on his bed and his nightshirt, to witness his own funeral, even to kneel down in the churchyard and trace with his fingers his name on the tombstone.

On Christmas Eve, Scrooge saw the light. Much of the good news of *A Christmas Carol* is that when Scrooge did see the light he didn't have to change jobs or leave town or enter the ministry. He just had to start treating people right, beginning with his clerk Bob Cratchit, and Cratchit's little sickly son, Tiny Tim. He had to begin seeing those around him not as a part of the landscape, not as people to be used, but as "fellow-passengers to the grave, and not another race of creatures bound on other journeys."

Conversion happens. There's always hope—even for a "covetous old sinner" like Ebenezer Scrooge.

Take a few minutes to reflect on what you've just read.

Chapter Forty-Five

One may have a blazing hearth in one's soul, and
yet no one ever comes to sit by it.

Vincent van Gogh

I met June twenty-something years ago when she
brought her only child, a ten-day-old baby boy, into
the emergency room. He had been, inexplicably, attacked
by the family pet. He died three days later. June, under-
standably, went into deep, immobilizing depression. Then
one day, many weeks later, she got up and had her hair
fixed in a different style. She began seeing an orthodon-
tist to straighten her teeth. She bought a new wardrobe.
She decided not to go back to her job as a supervisor in a
fast-food restaurant, where she had been very successful,
but to enroll in college.

Something else was going on in June at a deeper level.
She began seeing others differently. She began doing vol-
unteer work in the chaplains' office. She became a coun-
selor in a support group for bereaved parents. She
produced a videotape to teach pediatricians how to help

bereaved parents. She spoke to medical residents and students on how to care for parents of a dying child.

Two years after her baby died, June began having balance problems. A large malignant tumor was found in her spinal column. Surgery to remove it left her partially paralyzed. It became clear that June was going to die soon. Several weeks before she died June gave me a Barry Manilow album with the instructions to play one song at her funeral as her final message to the world. The song was titled "I Made It through the Rain." The line she liked most was one about respect earned from other people who "got rained on too."

June died over twenty years ago. Every year since then, a few days before Christmas, I get a call from the operator at our local children's hospital that a big package for me has arrived. It's a box of toys and gifts, provided by June's will, to be delivered to sick and dying children who are stuck in the hospital over Christmas.

Hope doesn't like to go it alone. Hope is social. It craves others to sit by its blazing hearth.

Use the space below to record your thoughts.

Chapter Forty-Six

YHWH

The only way out is through, and our choice is whether we shall cringe from it or affirm it.

Rollo May

Does anything put hope to the test more than terminal illness or bereavement? Or what about war or starvation? What if all four came to one home bundled together? Is hope still a choice?

Consider Martin Rinkart. Rinkart was a seventeenth-century Lutheran pastor. His first church call was to a congregation in his Saxony hometown. The beginning of his pastorate coincided with the beginning of the Thirty Years' War in Europe. In addition to the ravages of war, Saxony was struck by the plague. The plague was followed by a famine. Martin Rinkart's wife and children died in the plague. He was the only one of the three pastors in town to survive. Over eight thousand citizens in his small walled town died. On some days Rinkart conducted over fifty funerals. It was at the end of one of those days, when it looked like the carnage would never end, that he sat down and penned these immortal words:

Now thank we all our God,
With heart and hands and voices,
Who wondrous things hath done,
In whom His earth rejoices.
Who from our mother's arm
Hath blessed us on our way
With countless gifts of love,
And still is ours today.

O may this bounteous God,
Through all our life be near us,
With ever joyful hearts,
And blessed peace to cheer us,
And keep us in His grace
And guide us when perplexed,
And free us from all ills,
In this world and the next.

All praise and thanks to God,
The Father, now be given,
The Son and Him who reigns,
With them in highest Heaven;
The one eternal God,
Whom earth and Heaven adore;
For thus it was, is now,
And shall be evermore!

Rickart's hymn of hope is living commentary on the truth of scripture: "We also boast in our sufferings, knowing that suffering produces endurance, and endurance produces character, and character produces hope, and hope does not disappoint us, because God's love has been poured into our hearts" (Rom. 5:3–5).

Take a few minutes to reflect on what you've just read.

Chapter Forty-Seven

Our main business is not to see what lies dimly at
a distance, but to do what lies clearly at hand.
Thomas Carlyle

One part of hope is having a goal and keeping an eye
on it. There's a harder part—the daily determination to keep moving doggedly toward it.

A century and a half ago, a popular sport in America
was pedestrianism, sometimes called professional walking, sometimes called ultra-marathoning. People speed-
walked over long distances. The all-time champion was
Edward Weston. In 1874 he walked 500 miles in 6 days.
When he turned 70, to celebrate his birthday he walked
from New York City to San Francisco—3,900 miles—in
105 days. When he turned 71, he walked from Los Angeles to New York City—3,300 miles—in 77 days. Imagine
the storms, the hail, the sleet and the heat, the mountains
and deserts he negotiated. Imagine getting up every day
and doing it all over again. Edward Weston died at age 90
in New York City. He was run over by a taxi.

"Pedestrian" has a derogatory connotation in our day. We call something pedestrian if it's common, boring, and repetitive. There's nothing exciting about putting one foot in front of the other a million times. That doesn't pack the thrill of seeing a sprinter blazing across the finish line in 9.2 seconds. But if a core value is stamina—endurance, persistence, staying on task, being faithful to a mission—pedestrianism is hope's best friend.

William Natcher was a civic ultra-marathoner. He was a Kentucky congressman for forty years. I've been told by several people whom I respect and who knew him well that he was the most ethical man they have ever known. He never once accepted a campaign contribution of any kind. He never once missed one vote in congress in forty years. Asked late in life what epitaph he would like on his grave marker, he replied that under his name and birth date and death date he would appreciate having six words engraved: *He Tried to Do It Right.*

Pedestrianism built the pyramids, cleared the wilderness, and puts bread in the grocery store. It is hope's unsung best friend.

Use the space below to record your thoughts.

Chapter Forty-Eight

Hope means to keep living amid desperation, and
to keep humming in the darkness.

Henri Nouwen

Hope is where you find it. Sometimes it presents
itself in the least likely people and places.

The most spiritually lean year of my life was 1967. The
Vietnam War was raging in all its horrors. Boys my age were
coming home with missing limbs or in body bags. Pessimism
permeated the country. The religion of my childhood was
failing me theologically, intellectually, and spiritually. I didn't
know what to believe or what I wanted to do with my life.

If someone had told me then that I would soon begin a
thirty-year career as a hospital chaplain, I would have
laughed. The bridge to that wonderful, fulfilling career
was a book written by a man who was not a churchman or
even a Christian—the French existentialist and agnostic,
Albert Camus.

In his novel *The Plague*, Camus chronicles the grotesque
sufferings that struck a small Algerian town in the 1940s.

The chronicler was a physician, Dr. Rieux, who tended lovingly to the plague's victims. Three sentences in *The Plague* stuck with me and spoke sense to my soul. One was attributed to a surviver of the plague: "On this earth there are pestilences and there are victims, and it's up to us, so far as possible, not to join forces with the pestilences." One came from Dr. Rieux: "I decided to take, in every predicament, the victim's side, so as to reduce the damage done." The novel ends with a call to those in the future (like me) who would find themselves caught up in "the never-ending fight against terror and its relentless onslaughts." It referred to us as those "who, while unable to be saints, but refusing to bow down to pestilences, strive their utmost to be healers."

Those ideas ("Get on the victim's side"; "Don't bow down to pestilences"; "If you can't be a saint, be a healer") resonated within me. It sounded much like the original way of Jesus, a way that easily gets lost in the rigmarole of religion. I decided that I could be a healer, and would leave sainthood and doctrinal wranglings to others.

Working to keep hope alive in a time of cholera is one way to try to construct a life that counts for something.

Use the space below to record your thoughts.

Chapter Forty-Nine

Bidden or unbidden, God is here.
Carl Jung

I've been amused for years at the concept of "invocation"—the idea that God needs to be "called in" at the beginning of a conference or a church service or a football game.

The old-time religion featured an old male god with fixed jaw and stern eyes and white hair, sitting on a distant throne. From time to time he would meddle in human affairs, sending a plague here or a cancer there, meting out punishment for sin from afar. If people wanted him to cut them some slack, they slaughtered goats or bulls and threw them on an altar, or they flagellated themselves. If they wanted good crops or a healing, they prayed long prayers or beat on drums or danced around a bonfire to try to persuade the remote god to have mercy and come on down.

There is an alternative understanding of God. It is sometimes called "incarnational theology" and is represented in the title Emmanuel—"God with us." Martin

Luther spoke of "God from the bottom upwards instead of from the top downwards." This is an understanding of God, not over fifteen billion light years away waiting to be called in, but the vibrant, unifying force at the molecular level, at the center of life.

Candace Pert, once chief of brain chemistry at the National Institutes of Health, conceives of God as "neuropeptides"—the means by which all things at the cellular level communicate and cohere. Dylan Thomas wrote, "The force that through the green fuse drives the flower drives my green age; the force that drives the sea water through the rocks drives my red blood." This God doesn't need to be coaxed to come down to us, and doesn't require many finely worded prayers before coming to our aid. This God is nearer to us than the air we breathe—sustaining, energizing, and healing us.

Carl Jung celebrated his knowledge of this friendly God—God present with us and for us—by keeping a saying over his office door. His family had the saying inscribed on his tombstone: *Vocatus atque non vocatus, Deus aderit.* "Bidden or unbidden, God is here."

Use the space below to record your thoughts.

Chapter Fifty

My purpose holds to sail beyond the sunset, and
the baths of all the western stars, until I die.
                                        Alfred Lord Tennyson

I clearly remember the first time I felt old. Can you? For
many of us it was a birthday that ended with a 0 or a 5.
For me, it came at the Indiana State Fair in Indianapolis
when I was 31 years young. There were in those days
carnies at the fair who guessed your weight or age, and if
they were a few years or pounds off, you won a stuffed animal. We were a little family of three then, and I desperately
wanted to win a stuffed dog for our 9-month-old baby.

Occasionally I was still being mistaken—at 31—for a
college student. Figuring I would be a cinch to win, I
plunked down my 75 cents. The age-guessing expert
looked me over, wrote down his guess on a pad, showed
his guess to the crowd, and asked my age. I told him 31.
Two things then happened simultaneously—a gasp went
up from the crowd, and the carnie dropped his jaw in dis-
belief. As he reached to get my stuffed dog, he showed me

his guess: 40. How would you feel if someone told you that you looked a decade older that you were? What chaffed most was the little pearl of advice that came with the stuffed animal. He quipped: "Partner, you need to lay off the hard stuff!"

As a "prematurely gray" person most of my life, I had to start thinking prematurely about aging. The position I ultimately staked out is capsuled in words from the apostle Paul: "We do not lose heart. Even though our outer nature is wasting away, our inner nature is being renewed day by day" (2 Cor. 4:16). What I must do is not lose heart, not become "leaden-eyed." I find Vachel Lindsay's words about the leaden-eyed haunting:

> Let not young souls be smothered out before
> They do quaint deeds and fully flaunt their pride.
> It is the world's one crime its babes grow dull,
> Its poor are ox-like, limp and leaden-eyed.
>
> Not that they starve, but starve so dreamlessly;
> Not that they sow, but that they seldom reap;
> Not that they serve, but have no gods to serve;
> Not that they die, but that they die like sheep.

Not to lose heart; to have eyes that sparkle and twinkle; to choose (in Tennyson's words) "to strive, to seek, to find, and not to yield"—however chronologically gifted we may be—is the trick.

Take a few minutes to reflect on what you've just read.

Chapter Fifty-One

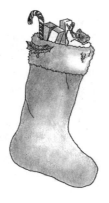

On.

Samuel Beckett

In some primal sense, hope is innate to all things living—plants, animals, humans—even unbelievers.

Two modern writers who argue forcefully for the absurdity and futility of life are nevertheless against suicide and for soldiering on.

Albert Camus examines Homer's myth of Sisyphus, who was sentenced by the gods to roll a boulder up a mountain. Every time Sisyphus got the boulder to the top, it rolled back down, and he would have to walk down to the bottom of the mountain and push it up to the top all over again—eternally. What a vivid, accurate snapshot of the human condition! So much of life is spent in the daily grind—difficult, tedious, repetitive, unsatisfying, meaningless, robotic work. What's the point? Why keep on? For what? To Camus, the *what* is heroic endurance. Sisyphus, on his trip down the hill, enjoys the cool breeze on his brow and is free to think. Camus concludes, "The struggle itself toward the heights is enough to fill a man's heart. We have to imagine Sisyphus happy."

Samuel Beckett, in *Waiting for Godot*, has two tramps, Estragen and Vladimir, waiting beside a tree for a Mr. Godot, whom they do not know. They don't know if they will recognize him if he does come. They pass the time. They use a variety of distractions to cope with their boredom and to deal with the fact that Godot doesn't show. They wait and wait, and nothing happens. The next day they begin their wait all over again. At one point Vladimir asked Pozzo, a blind man who came by, "Where do you go from here?" Blind Pozzo replied, "On."

Much of life is boring and unfulfilling. Much is spent waiting for something to happen or someone to intervene to make it better. The play insinuates that going *on* in hope, like blind Pozzo, is heroic—whether Godot ever comes or not.

We are hardwired for hope. Even the futilists' last word is *on*.

Use the space below to record your thoughts.

Chapter Fifty-Two

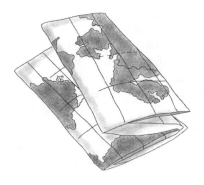

I steer my bark with Hope in the head, leaving
Fear astern.

Thomas Jefferson

When mapmakers of old came to the end of the
known world, they drew a fire-breathing dragon.
The symbol of the dragon shouted grave danger:
"Beware! You may fall off the world if you venture past
here! You may get lost and never find your way back! You
may get devoured by a giant sea monster!"

Life for most of us is a lot like that—a treacherous voyage across an ominous, uncharted sea.

Two of our first three presidents, Thomas Jefferson and
John Adams, likened their lives to a sea voyage. Adams had
defeated Jefferson in the 1796 presidential election, and
Jefferson had defeated Adams in 1800. Even so, in the last
fourteen years of their lives they became fast friends and
exchanged many letters. When they were both in their
seventies, Adams asked Jefferson in a letter if he would
want to live life over again. Jefferson, who had lost his wife

Patty from complications following childbirth and never married again, whose second child lived less than two years and whose only son lived less than a month, replied, "It is a good world on the whole. . . . I steer my bark with Hope in the head, leaving Fear astern."

Picking up Jefferson's seafaring metaphor, Adams replied, "I admire your navigation and should like to sail with you, either in your bark or in my own, along side of yours—Hope with her bright-colored Ensigns displayed at the Prow, fear with her Hobgoblins behind the Stern."

Jefferson, whose place in the history books as the architect of American democracy was secure, closed his next letter with this declaration: "I like the dreams of the future better than the history of the past. So good night. I will dream on."

In one of history's great ironies, Jefferson and Adams, full of years, completed their voyage three hours apart on the same day, July 4, 1826, exactly fifty years after the signing of the Declaration of Independence.

Hope, like fear, is a choice. Regardless of circumstances, we choose to sail our vessel with "Hope and her bright-colored Ensigns" or "Fear and her Hobgoblins" going before us. Which way makes for a better life? A better world? Which way produces the kind of people we like to be around, and want around us?

So, good night! I will dream on.

Take a few minutes to reflect on what you've just read.